Charles William Super, Henri Weil

The Order of Words in the Ancient Languages

Compared with that of the modern languages

Charles William Super, Henri Weil

The Order of Words in the Ancient Languages
Compared with that of the modern languages

ISBN/EAN: 9783337085186

Printed in Europe, USA, Canada, Australia, Japan

Cover: Foto ©Paul-Georg Meister /pixelio.de

More available books at **www.hansebooks.com**

THE ORDER OF WORDS

IN THE

ANCIENT LANGUAGES COMPARED WITH THAT
OF THE MODERN LANGUAGES.

BY

HENRI WEIL.

Translated, with Notes and Additions,

BY

CHARLES W. SUPER, Ph.D.,
PRESIDENT OF THE OHIO UNIVERSITY.

"*Language is an art and a glorious one, whose influence extends over all others, and in which finally all science whatever must centre.*"

BOSTON:
GINN & COMPANY, PUBLISHERS.
1887.

INTRODUCTION TO THE TRANSLATION.

THE English-speaking student who enters upon the study of an ancient language is soon led to ask, "Why is the order of words to which I am accustomed so different from this? and why does an ancient writer put his thoughts together in a way that seems so unnatural?" When he comes to the German he finds its arrangement a little less unusual; while if he undertakes the French he soon discovers far more points of agreement than dissimilarity between the new language and his own. There may be nothing surprising to him in the fact that hardly any two languages designate the same object with precisely the same term; but why should the component parts of a complex thought be arranged so differently with respect to one another? We read what Greek and Roman and Hebrew and German thinkers have said upon all questions of general human interest and see nothing foreign in their ideas. There is no ancient history, or philosophy, that is materially unlike in its principles what is called modern history, or modern philosophy. When we have extracted the ideas from the unfamiliar words and their strange arrangement, we find nothing about them which, generally speaking, impresses us as strange. We must conclude, then, that the human mind is the same in all ages, where the civilization is virtually on the same level. In poetic composition it is easy to see why words cannot be arranged in the same order when a thought in different languages is expressed in words of different lengths and differently accented. In prose, the reason of the divergence is much more difficult to discover.

Perhaps no one would maintain that any amount of research will ever make it possible to account for the minor divergences of speech. Countless idiomatic expressions owe their existence to circumstances entirely beyond the reach of even plausible divination. Stereotyped formulas are repeated by each succeeding generation of the unthinking multitude in whose mouths the inheritance receives no increment. With it speech is not really the expression of thought; it is hardly more than the verbal utterance of concepts called into existence by impressions on the sensorium from without. But even under such conditions language is an object of interest as the tangible and visible form of national or tribal feeling: the interest is a far higher and nobler one when it concerns language which is something more than a mere inheritance, and which has become a vehicle of new thoughts called into being in a mind conscious of its power and capable of moulding these thoughts into forms that will impress themselves ineffaceably upon human civilization.

A well-known English author says that nothing can be more evident than that custom makes the Briton prefer one order of words and the Frenchman another. This is only removing the difficult point one degree further back. We may well ask, accepting the statement as true, what makes custom in such a case; for it is coming to be more and more admitted among students of sociology that no custom is purely arbitrary. If there is no reason for it now apparent or discoverable, it has survived by tradition after the cause which called it into existence ceased to be operative. Several French writers have maintained that their language follows the natural order in the arrangement of words. The same claims have been put forth by writers of other nationalities in behalf of their vernacular; nor is there any real difference between these and the theories about the languages spoken in Paradise. We are led to conclude that the question of the order of words has been rarely approached in a philosophical spirit, and that it has been generally decided on purely subjective grounds. Though the dead languages have been carefully studied during the last three or four centuries, I am not aware that much has been done toward a systematic and thorough examination of the question which is the theme of the present volume. The consideration of the subject is confined pretty generally to a single author or to one work of an author, and is not pursued upon a sufficiently comprehensive plan to lead to results capable of wide or universal application. Most students, I am led to believe, complete their collegiate course in the ancient languages, in the firm belief that there is an irreconcilable difference between ancient and modern modes of expression; and that the divergences can be referred to no general principles.

But the question of the order of words as determined by the order of the ideas of which they are the visible and audible expression, has not only a philosophical interest, but a pedagogical value also. Every time a student carefully and appreciatively examines a sentence left on record by a thoughtful writer of antiquity, he receives a lesson in vigorous and systematic thinking. If he recognizes the psychological kinship between his own mind and the mind that speaks to him from the written page out of the remote depths of antiquity, and through the agency of a foreign idiom, he must be dull indeed if the discovery does not delight his soul, cultivate his intellect, and enlarge his mental horizon.

Having for a good many years been aware of the existence of the confusion and uncertainty in the minds of students, of which I have above spoken, and not knowing where to direct them for an authoritative guide in the investigation of the order of words, I was greatly delighted when some years ago I found in the little work of Professor Weil, of Paris, a lucid and systematic introduction to the study of the whole question. Even if we dissent from his conclusions in part or in whole, we cannot read his book without being stimulated to further research, and led to entertain the belief that the order of words in the ancient languages is not so much unlike the modern as is commonly supposed. The fact that so eminent a philologist has seen no reason to change his views after a study of the subject extending through nearly two score years, ought to convince any one that they cannot be easily overthrown. But I am less concerned about convincing my readers than about stimulating them to thought upon a question of so much importance. If I have aroused investigation and indicated a method which will lead to fruitful results, I care not at all whether the results of others' studies correspond with mine. I had far rather they should differ *toto coelo*, if in that way the cause of truth be the more promoted.

The author's notes I have in nearly all cases marked with the signature W. A very few I have omitted where their retention seemed of no importance to the English reader. Here and there I have added a line or a word in the text when this brief explanation obviated the necessity of a note. In a few cases I have incorporated a note by the author into the text where this seemed to me an improvement. Many of the quotations from the Greek and the Latin are given without translation in the original work. Besides, as the French translation, where the author has added one, would be of little value to the English reader, I have in many cases omitted it and supplied its place with an English translation. Where the author's words would be of interest to those who read French, I have retained them enclosed in brackets. In all cases where it seemed advisable I have supplied an English version, whether a French one was given or not. Where a suitable one was within reach, I used it; where not, — and this was the case in a majority of instances, — I made one or changed another's to suit my purpose. Some who will read these pages could doubtless have made better; a large number will perhaps think they could do so until they have themselves made the trial.

As the class of readers for which the translation is intended is less learned than that for which the original was prepared, there was need of a considerable number of notes by the translator. Some were also rendered necessary by the change in the point of view from French to English. It has been no easy matter to decide how numerous or how long to make them. The thesis touches upon many points of interest to philologists; but how many of these by-paths, frequently so alluring, one ought here to follow, and how far to follow them, are questions upon which there will probably be a wide divergence of opinion. I have been guided by what I regarded as the needs of the class for which the translation is primarily intended.

If this little work contributes anything toward removing the obstacles that lie in the path of the student of the ancient classic tongues; especially if it enables him to see design and symmetry where he has found only chance and irregularity; if, in short, it makes the study of the noblest languages of antiquity, in however slight a degree, more attractive, more profitable intellectually, and more humanizing, the object of the translator will be fully attained. And I doubt not that of the author also.

I ought perhaps to add that the translation has been made under circumstances of no small difficulty. The frequent interruptions due to the claims of a laborious position left but snatches of time for any self-imposed task. This fact does not detract from the intrinsic merit of the performance, but it may account for minor errors and for some defects of style that would not have been overlooked under more favorable conditions.

I desire to express my grateful acknowledgments to Professor J. B. Greenough, of Harvard University, for valuable suggestions, and to my colleague Professor J. P. Gordy, for his generous aid in reading the proofs.

C. W. S.

ATHENS, O., January, 1887.

TABLE OF CONTENTS.

	PAGE
INTRODUCTION TO THE TRANSLATION	3
PREFACE	9
INTRODUCTION BY THE AUTHOR	11
Notes	17

CHAPTER I.

The Principle of the Order of Words	21
The Syntactic March is not the March of Ideas	21
An Attempt to set forth the March of Ideas	28
Applications of the General Remarks	31
Modifications of the Principle of the Order of Words	35
The Pathetic Order of Words	43
Notes	47

CHAPTER II.

The Relation between the Order of Words and the Syntactic Form of the Proposition	52
Classification of Languages according to Construction	52
Place of the Verb	57
Descending and Ascending Construction	59
What is the most Perfect Construction?	67
Construction in the Free Languages	70
The Period	74
Notes	79

CHAPTER III.

The Relation between Words and the Rhetorical Accent	85
Ascending Accentuation	87
Descending Accentuation	93
Repose of Emphasis	100
Oratorical Rhythm	108
False Emphasis	109
Notes	111

PREFACE.

Since the appearance of the second edition of this work, M. Abel Bergaigne has published the beginning of a study on *grammatical construction considered in its historical development in Sanskrit, Greek, Latin, the Romanic and Germanic languages*.[1] M. Bergaigne attempts with as much learning as ingenuity to determine the primitive usage in matters of grammatical construction with respect to the idioms which are the object of his researches; and going still farther back to discover by conjecture the arrangement of the constituent parts of the proposition in the mother tongue of the Indo-European family. On the other hand, M. G. von der Gabelentz has published some articles on *comparative syntax*.[2] Among the facts gathered by this linguist, I regard as particularly interesting those pertaining to the function of the particle *fa* in the Japanese language. In his general views upon the principle of the order of words there is nothing that I did not point out twenty-five years before him. The results of neither of these investigations has led to a change in my own views. That of von der Gabelentz has added nothing of importance, whereas Bergaigne's point of view is wholly different.

Excepting some slight retouches of style, this third edition is an exact reproduction of the second (1869), which in its turn differed from the first (1844) only in a few modifications and additions. It would have been easy to extend the little work, but its conciseness has perhaps counted for something in the favorable reception that has been accorded to it. I refrain therefore from adding any additional matter. It were to be wished in the interest of readers, that writers should take for a motto, Μέγα βιβλίον μέγα κακόν.

Paris, June, 1879.

[1] *Mémoires de la Société de Linguistique de Paris*, Vol. III, p. 1 seqq., p. 124 seqq., p. 109 seqq.

[2] *Ideen zu einer vergleichenden Syntax* in *Zeitschrift für Völkerpsychologie*. Vol. VI, p. 376 seqq., and Vol VIII, p. 129 seqq., p. 300 seqq.

THE ORDER OF WORDS

IN THE

ANCIENT LANGUAGES COMPARED WITH THE MODERN.

AUTHOR'S INTRODUCTION.

It is proposed in this essay to treat of the order in which words or groups of words that are used in the formation of a sentence may properly follow each other. Words are the signs of ideas; to treat of the order of words is, then, in a measure, to treat of the order of ideas. From this point of view our subject has a claim to be regarded as one of some importance. Grammarians have very carefully studied isolated words, as also their syntactical concatenation; but most of them have given no attention to the order in which words may follow each other. Nevertheless the study of this order would seem to be a considerable part of grammar, for the object of grammar is to explain how thought is translated into words. Thought is in perpetual movement; the forward movement of speech cannot then be reasonably ignored.

Before entering upon our subject, let us glance rapidly over what both ancient and modern writers have said upon it. Among the former, Dionysius of Halicarnassus has devoted a special treatise to σύνθεσις ὀνομάτων; Cicero in the Orator, and in his other writings on rhetoric, and Quintilian in his *Institutiones Oratoriae*, treat at length of *compositio verborum*. They all agree in acknowledging the importance of this subject. Dionysius goes even so far as to claim that the choice of words is not of as much consequence as the order in which they are placed. That which should determine this order, according to the ancient rhetoricians, is the more or less harmonious collocation of the letters placed at the end or the beginning of the words which follow each other; the rhythmic movement produced by the succession of long and short syllables, which they call respectively *conglutinatio verborum* and *numerus;* and finally reasons of euphony of which the ear alone is a competent judge.

If this were true, if in reality the order of words were entirely, or almost entirely, a matter which concerns the ear, as the most respectable authorities assert, it would be better to exclude the Greek and the Latin from these researches. We do not know the exact pronunciation of these languages; we reproduce it even less than we know it. Besides, euphony varies with the organs and habits of peoples. What is agreeable to the French ear is not always so to the English or German ear: the more reason then why a collection of words considered harmonious in our day could not have been so to Cicero or Pericles. We are therefore as badly situated as possible for judging the euphony of a Greek or Latin sentence. Nevertheless it cannot be denied that those who are versed in the ancient languages feel the peculiar charm resulting from the arrangement of the sentence by the classic prose writers. What is more, we moderns try to imitate them, and pride ourselves upon being able to write more or less well the language of Cicero or Demosthenes. Of two things one must be true: either there is a very extraordinary blindness among modern writers, or the ancient masters of the oratorical art have not sought out and unravelled all the causes of this arrangement — an arrangement the appositeness of which they had such an exquisitely keen perception. It will be surmised that any one who undertakes to determine the principles of this arrangement should incline toward the latter opinion. It is doubtless somewhat venturesome to pretend to be a better judge of Greek or Latin than Dionysius or Cicero; but it is less so than one might suppose at first sight. It happens every day that men who possess a certain art in its fullest perfection, who have the keenest and justest judgment in all that relates thereto, expound the processes of this art in a much less satisfactory manner than those who seek to render themselves masters of it by study. The former judge in such matters by their feelings, or, in other words, by a method that is sufficiently reliable in practice, but confusing in theory; the latter judge by the understanding, which is insufficient, perhaps, in practice, but which is excellent in theory. We rarely take pains to think out the reason of those things with which we are so familiar as not to be easily mistaken, but we study thoroughly those things which we can only learn by study. This is my apology for daring to maintain that the ancients have not always sufficiently fathomed the secret laws of an art which they apply as masters.

Let us try to prove by an example the statement we have just made. Cicero in the 64th chapter of the Orator cites the following passage taken from a speech of the tribune C. Carbo, *O Marce Druse, patrem appello. Tu dicere solebas sacram esse rempublicam, quicumque eam violavissent, ab omnibus esse ei poenas persolutas. Patris dictum sapiens temeritas filii comprobavit*.[1] And he adds, "The cadence of this sentence ending in a double trochee, gained for the orator the most vociferous applause." I ask whether it was not the rhetorical harmony that gained the applause. Change the order of the words and say, *e.g.*, *comprobavit filii temeritas* — it will no longer have the same effect, yet the words are the same, the sense is the same. We answer that it is because the mind is satisfied, but the ear is not. Cicero has elsewhere called attention to the fact that what is called rhythm in prose is not always produced by verse properly so called.[2] This remark can readily be turned against its author. In the first place it is very certain that the order of the words *comprobavit filii temeritas* does not offend the ear in the least. Thus changed, the sentence ends in a paeon, a rhythm or foot which Cicero elsewhere recommends, and which Aristotle and others put in the front rank. We are thus fully convinced that it is neither the paeon nor the dichoreus which makes this turn of the sentence languid, and that grand. It is not the rhythm of the syllables, but the order of ideas which produces this effect. By placing the verb at the end, as Carbo has done, the sentence is rounded out, and the contrary terms *sapiens* and *temeritas* are pitted against each other. The prudence of the father, the rashness of the son, — what is the relation that exists between these contrary terms? Have they joined in conflict, destroyed each the other? No; *comprobavit*, one has proven and confirmed the other. We do not deny, however, that the judgment of the ear is an important factor in the arrangement of the sentence; but we believe that this judgment of the ear conceals a judgment of the understanding.

The order of the words, submitted in this way to the approval of the ear, does not come, properly speaking, within the province of the grammarian. Nevertheless we see already in ancient times a disposition among grammarians, though somewhat feebly manifested, to devote themselves to this very important part of language. We see some of them, even in the face of common usage, applying themselves to the fixing of laws which had appeared to them the only logical and natural ones. Dionysius of Halicarnassus takes credit to himself for the invention of an artificial system, which may however be borrowed from some more ancient grammarian. According to this system,[3] substantives, as expressing substance, should precede verbs, which express only accident; verbs again ought to be placed before adverbs, for, says he, action in its nature precedes circumstances of manner, place, time, etc.; adjectives ought to follow substances; the indicative ought to precede the other modes, etc. But the Greek rhetorician makes haste to add that this theory, although specious, is refuted by experience; that no importance must be attached to it, and that it is of no real value. Quintilian makes mention of the same system, but he likewise rejects it as too artificial, and as contrary to experience. Nevertheless the grammarians do not entirely give up these theories. The author of the treatise *De Elocutione* recommends the order of words which he calls natural (φυσικὴ τάξις), and he does not speak of substantives and verbs, but has in view, to judge from his expressions, what are called subject and attribute.[4] This rhetorician uses exaggerated expressions to establish a theory which he has not himself practised in the treatise which contains it. He thinks that every proposition which does not begin with the subject, lacks clearness, and puts to the rack the speaker no less than the hearer. Hermogenes seems to apply to the rhetorical period this same analytical principle when he speaks of a direct order and an indirect order.

These theories, which, as may be seen, are those of modern

grammarians, do not appear to have been much developed among the ancients. One fact, however, could not escape the attention of any who have reflected upon language: it frequently happens both in Greek and Latin that words are separated which evidently form together a syntactical group. This accident of language must of necessity have been observed as soon as men had observed in languages the existence of genders, numbers, cases, and terminations, which serve to express these relations. In fact the technical term *hyperbaton* is invariably used by Plato in the same sense which has attached to it ever since. It cannot be doubted that the ancient sophists were the first to make this grammatical observation, and Plato borrowed the term from his adversaries.[5] It is pretty well known that the moderns have formulated into a general rule the theory that was rejected by Dionysius of Halicarnassus and Quintilian. The requirements of teaching, the genius of our language, perhaps also the analytical tendency of our minds, have made the fortune of this theory. The first persons who entered a little more deeply into the question of the order of words were not as one would naturally suppose the learned authors of Greek and Latin grammars, but those who have treated of modern languages. This fact is not without importance. It appears that the order of words is closely bound up with the life of a language; that it holds to the spoken word, and not to the written letter. The longest and most animated discussion pertaining to this topic, that has ever arisen, was that carried on in the eighteenth century between Beauzée and the Abbé Batteux.[6] These worthy savans without doubt possessed sufficient intelligence to solve this problem, or at least to lay the foundations of a general theory of the order of words. If they did not succeed, it was perhaps because they had made a question of grammar to be a question of party; because they set out to establish by their debate the superiority of the French language or of the ancient languages. Beauzée confines himself to the system of syntax which he knew how to develop in his grammar with so much logic. He refuses to follow his adversary on any other ground. We shall have occasion further on to cite some of the most striking passages in his chapter on construction. Batteux thinks that the natural arrangement of the parts of a sentence consists in always placing the most important idea at the head, that is, in the most prominent part of the sentence, and in always giving to the ideas which represent a greater interest the precedence over those which represent a less. It is evident that he regards that order as natural which is called the pathetic, the order of great emotion. He appears to suppose that the grammatical or metaphysical order — in fine, the French order — is always the exact opposite of the natural order, the order of the Latin. According to him, the farther we depart from the legitimate arrangement of the French sentence, the better we speak. He professes to believe that *rotundus est sol* is better than *sol est rotundus;* to hear *filius amat patrem* would have sounded as harsh to the Romans as to us the order, "by the son is loved the father." One sees that this savant allows himself to be so far carried away in the heat of the discussion as to ignore the differences of languages, and to advance a theory that cannot be sustained; but he had a keen perception of the beauty and advantages of the Latin construction, nor did he fail to make some very good observations upon it.

The first really philosophical grammars of the German language could not avoid discussing the construction of this language, a construction which is determined by the syntactical relations of the parts of the proposition, but which does not follow the analytical order. Herling and Becker[7] have treated this part of their subject with the same profoundness as the other parts of grammar. They have not confined themselves to establishing the usual construction of the German, but they have sought the reasons of the different inversions. They have called particular attention to the fact that there exists an intimate relation between accentuation and the order of words.[8] Although I have felt obliged to take issue with these grammarians in seeking a principle that regulates the order of words independent of syntax, I am glad to recognize the fact that their works first gave me light upon this subject and led me to reflect upon it.

Among the works which treat specifically of the Latin construction I shall cite but two, the only ones that I have myself been able to read. Dr. R. Stürenburg in the notes which he has added to an oration of Cicero — that for the poet Archias — has sought to explain the arrangement of the Latin sentence by the emphasis. He distinguishes four kinds of emphasis, — a grammatical, a logical, an emphatic, and, fourthly, an emphasis which results from emotion intentionally restrained. The grammatical emphasis gives the usual order of words. A word which is affected either by the logical or grammatical emphasis is placed before the rest; a word which has the restrained emphasis is placed after the others. Dr. F. Raspe has appended to his edition of Cicero *de Legibus* a treatise on the order of words in Latin, in which he develops a theory proposed by Goerenz in his commentaries on several works of Cicero. This theory makes us acquainted with a particular *sonus* possessed by the Latin language, which rests upon the first, the fourth, the seventh, and the last word of each proposition. I confess that in spite of my efforts I have not been able to comprehend this theory.

---

[1] The section here referred to is perhaps of sufficient importance to merit a place entire. *Fluit omnino numerus a primo tum incitatius brevitate pedum, tum proceritate tardius. Cursum contentiones magis requirunt; expositiones rerum, tarditatem. Insistit autem ambitus modis pluribus, e quibus unam est secuta Asia maxime, qui dichoreus vocatur, quam duo extremi chorei sunt, id est, e singulis longis et brevibus; explanandum est enim, quod ab aliis iidem pedes aliis nominantur vocabulis. Dichoreus non est ille quidem sua sponte vitiosus in clausulis, sed in orationis numero nihil est tam vitiosum, quam si semper est idem. Cadit autem per se ille ipse praeclare; quo etiam satietas formidanda est magis, me stante C. Carbo, C. F. tribunus plebis in concione dixit his verbis,*

O Marce Druse, patrem appello. Haec quidem duo binis pedibus incisim: dein membratim, *tu dicere solebas sacram esse rempublicam. Haec item membra ternis. Post ambitus,*

quicumque violavissent, ab omnibus esse ei poenas persolutas. Dichoreus: nihil enim ad rem, extrema illa, longa sit, an brevis. Deinde,

Patris dictum sapiens, temeritas filii comprobavit. Hoc dichoreo tantus clamor concionis excitatus est, ut admirabile esset. Quaero, nonne id numerus effecerit? Verborum ordinem immuta: fac sic comprobavit filii temeritas: jam nihil erit, etsi temeritas ex tribus brevibus, et longa est; quem Aristoteles ut optimum probat; a quo dissentio. At eadem verba, eadem sententia. Animo istuc satis est, auribus non satis. Sed id crebrius fieri non oportet. Primum enim est numerus agnoscitur: deinde satiat: postea cognita facilitate contemnitur.

[2] See note [9], p. 113, and compare H. Spencer's Essay on the Origin and Function of Music.

³ De Compositione Verborum, chap. 5. Τὰ ὀνόματα τάττειν πρὸ τῶν ῥημάτων. It is incorrect to translate, as has often been done, "to place the subject before the verb." In reality, Aristotle (de Interpretatione, chap. 5) uses the term ὄνομα solely to designate the nominative, which he distinguishes from the oblique cases or πτώσεις ὀνόματος; but Dionysius proves by his examples (μῆνιν ἄειδε, the first words of the Iliad) that he does not make this distinction. It is possible that he did not fully comprehend the author from whom he borrowed his ideas. An analogous passage from Priscian makes one suspect this. This grammarian says (Institutiones Grammaticae XVII): *Sciendam tamen quod recta ordinatio exigit, ut pronomen vel nomen praeponatur verbo, ut ego et tu legimus, Virgilius et Cicero scripserunt, quippe cum substantia et persona ipsius agentis vel patientis, quae per pronomen vel nomen significatur, prior esse debet naturaliter quam ipse actus, qui accidens est substantiae. Licet tamen et praepostere ea proferre auctorum usurpatione fretum.* When we compare with this extract the terms used by Dionysius in the following, Τὰ μὲν γὰρ (ὀνόματα) τὴν οὐσίαν δηλοῦν τὰ δὲ (ῥήματα) τὸ συμβεβηκός· πρότερον δ' εἶναι τῇ φύσει τὴν οὐσίαν τῶν συμβεβηκότων, we are led to conclude that the two authors have drawn from the same source. W.

⁴ Demetrius, de Elocutione, Walz. Rhetores Graeci, p. 564: Τὸ περὶ οὗ, the thing spoken of. Ἤτοι ἀπὸ τῆς ὀρθῆς ἀρκτέον, ἢ ἀπὸ τῆς αἰτιατικῆς ὡς τὸ λέγεται Ἐπίδαμνον . . ., one must begin either with the nominative or the accusative in sentences in which the infinitive is construed with the subject of the accusative. W. The topics touched upon in these notes will be found fully discussed in Lersch, Die Sprachphilosophie der Alten, Bonn 1838–40; Steinthal, Geschichte der Sprachwissenschaft bei den Griechen und Römern, Berlin 1863. See also, Max Müller's Science of Language, First Series, Lecture III, and the article Grammar by Professor Sayce in the Encyclopedia Britannica.

⁵ For the grammarians of the Middle Age, see Thurot, *Extraits de divers manuscrits latins pour servir à l'histoire des doctrines grammaticales du moyen âge*, p. 341 ff. For Plato's use of the term *hyperbaton*, see Protagoras, p. 343 E. It is to the hyperbaton that the explanations of the ancient scholiasts refer which begin with these established formulas: *ordo est, τὸ ἑξῆς*. These interpreters only bring together the elements of the grammatical group. This is still a long remove from our analytical constructions.

⁶ Beauzée, *Grammaire générale*, Paris 1767. Batteux, *Traité de la construction oratoire*, 1763, and *Principes de literature*, 1774. See also Dumarsais, *Encyclopédie*, under the articles Languages, Construction; and Spencer's Essay on Style.

⁷ Herling, Die Syntax der deutschen Sprache, 2 Bde, 1830; K. F. Becker, Ausführliche deutsche Grammatik, 2 Bde, 1836–39.

Dr. Stürenburg's work was published in 1830; that of Dr. Raspe in 1844. An excellent chapter on the order of words in Latin is found in Reisig's Lateinische Sprachwissenschaft. A new edition of Haase's edition of this standard treatise is now (1886) in course of publication under the joint editorship of Schmalz and Landgraf. Some judicious remarks upon the same subject are to be found in the Handbuch der class. Alterthumswissenschaft now appearing from the press of Beck, Nördlingen. For Pronunciation the English reader may consult A. J. Ellis' Practical Hints on the Quantitative Pronunciation of Latin and the first vol. of Roby's Latin Grammar.

[8] The word "accent" embraces the meaning of both accent and emphasis. The French rhetoricians, however, speak of two kinds of accent, the tonic and the oratorical or pathetic accent. Their term being more comprehensive than ours, it is sometimes difficult to decide whether it had better be rendered by accent or by emphasis. The word 'accent' is formally the Latin word *accentus*, less its termination, which in turn is a literal translation of the Greek προσῳδία. But the signification of the modern word is not that of its ancient prototype. *Accentus*, from *accino*, is literally the attuning of a thing. It is composed of *ad* and *cantus*, just as its Greek equivalent is formed from πρός and ᾠδή. Quintilian and other Roman rhetoricians, however, mention the fact that Latin is less musical than Greek, whence it follows that the *accentus* of the one cannot have been precisely the same thing as the προσῳδία of the other. Its modern representative of course means something quite different.

CHAPTER I.

THE PRINCIPLE OF THE ORDER OF WORDS.

The syntactic march is not the march of ideas.

LET us forget for a moment the constructions peculiar to the French, German, English, Greek; let us rid ourselves of all that we know of the variations in the usage of one language as compared with another, and let us ask ourselves, what principle, judging by simple common sense, ought to regulate the order of words. We answer, because we try to trace in words the faithful image of thought, the order of words ought to reproduce the order of ideas; these two orders ought to be identical.

This principle I adopt fully, and shall try to develop it in this chapter. But, though adopting it, I do not understand it as many grammarians have done. It has often been invoked by them to prove that the analytical construction which is characteristic of several modern languages, and especially of the French, is the only one which corresponds to the order of our ideas.[1] I am not willing to admit this claim, either for this language or any other, and I believe that with slight modifications the signs of our ideas are always presented in the order of our ideas, and that the differences which have been cited are for the most part only seeming differences.

When grammarians speak of the order of ideas they have in mind the order of the constituent parts of the proposition as exhibited by syntactic analysis. The subject, the attribute, the different complements[2] of both, are the basis of all syntax. They constitute a system which applies equally to all languages, a thread which serves as a guide through all the most complicated constructions. Why, we shall be asked, not hold to a system so general, so transparent? Why not admit the fact that this system reveals to us in itself the forward movement of our ideas, and that consequently it is the **natural** basis of the order of words? We can answer this question only **after** we have examined the theory of the proposition itself.

Although all may be agreed when in a given case it is required to determine the parts of a proposition, it seems to me that we may distinguish two different methods of stating the fact. Sometimes we wish to express general propositions, such as, virtue is a good, vice is an evil. Then it is said, the proposition is the complete expression of a judgment (this is the definition of Beauzée). It naturally falls into two parts, a thing and a mode of being, between which we wish to establish a relation of agreement or disagreement. These two parts are the subject and the attribute. We are obliged to express first the subject and then the attribute under penalty of violating the logical order.

Sometimes we attach more importance to the sensible actions, which are expressed in most propositions and of which the relations are indicated by cases in inflected languages and by prepositions. Looked at in this light the subject is the person or thing from which the action proceeds, the verb is the expression of the action, the objects are the persons or things upon which the action is directed. *Darium vicit Alexander*. From whom does the action proceed? Begin where the action begins, namely, with Alexander. Darius is the person toward whom the action is directed. Place the name of Darius last. The verb which expresses the relation of the two persons, the manner in which the one acts upon the other, is the middle term, and ought to be placed between the others. Say then, "Alexander conquered Darius," under penalty of sinning against nature. By saying *Darium vicit Alexander*, you reverse natural order. To use the words of Beauzée, " you go from the end to the beginning, from the last term to the origin, from the bottom to the top; you invert nature quite as much as a painter who should exhibit the picture of a tree with the root above and the leaves in the earth. By saying *Darium Alexander vicit*, you depart even more from the natural order, you break the connection, you bring together the parts that have no affinity, as if by mere chance."

These arguments, one must admit, are at the same time very

simple and very forcible. Still, in the end, one is astonished to see the ancients convicted of being deficient in logic, and especially of being less natural than the moderns. The ancients, we may add in extenuation, had all the varied terminations by means of which they were able to find in their sentences the different parts even when they were widely dispersed. This is a weak excuse if it be really true that the order which is common in our language is the only logical and natural one. That you are rich and have the means to spend extravagantly without impairing your fortune is no reason why you should not be censured if you do so. Besides, if the ancients had inflections, we have prepositions, and in French, as in English, it is in truth only the nominative and accusative which are so much alike that they might cause confusion if the adopted order be widely departed from.[3] Let us examine, then, the force of the arguments upon which the generally received opinion rests. The proposition is the complete expression of a judgment, the two parts of which ought never to be confounded, but to follow each other regularly according to the logical order exhibited in the operations of the human mind. This is the first argument. It is true that one can reduce to the form of a judgment all that we say, and when there was given to this *ensemble* of words forming complete sense the somewhat unphilosophical name of proposition, it was perhaps done from this point of view. And more, our modern languages, in accord with our grammarians, tend to give their sentences the form of a judgment. These languages, including even the German, which is however tolerably free in respect to the order of its words, are especially careful to divide the sentence into two very distinct parts, between which is placed the copula as the sign of equation. We shall return hereafter to this philosophical, or rather, mathematical, conformation of the sentence which has become customary with us. But is it essential to the nature of language? Can we say that the function of the subject consists in being the object of a judgment expressed by the attribute? If you say, *Hunc juvenem intemperantia perdidit*, you do not express a judgment on intemperance, but simply state a fact; and if it is absolutely necessary that this should be a judgment, it is more natural to say that you express a judgment on the young man, who, however, is not the subject of the sentence. The same observation may be applied to a great number of sentences. The subject has not, therefore, and certainly had not originally, this philosophical value which our grammarians give to it and which our modern languages seem to affect for it. Hence the pattern after which all our sentences are modelled and which has shaped grammatical forms, is not primitively that of a judgment or of an algebraic equation.

The second argument proceeds, it seems to me, from a more correct point of view. According to it the subject is not the first term of a judgment, but the being from which the action proceeds: the other parts of the proposition are the term which enunciates this action, the object upon which it passes over, the circumstances of time, of place, etc. Finally, the entire proposition has the form of a sensible action. Nothing could better co-ordinate with the other facts of a language and with the nature of the mind which we must suppose to have existed in man before the formation of languages. Etymology is coming more and more to discover in the verbs the roots of all the other words in the language.[4] It appears then that man placed in the midst of this world so well calculated to impress his senses, first directed his attention to the changes, the movements, the actions, in a word, which are brought to his notice. Movement has awakened our first thoughts; we should not be surprised to see the form of our thoughts ascend to the same source, and to find in sensible action the prototype of the proposition. There is nothing more gratifying to the intelligence than to find the vocabulary and the syntax of our languages proceeding from the same source.

Of course it is not always a sensible action, often it is not an action at all that we express. But we are not here concerned about the content of a thought; it is only a question of its form, of the connection and syntactical relation of its parts. One can express a mode of being only by using the form employed in sentences which express action. We say, "The lion is a beast with a mane," "This man has talent," exactly as we say, "The lion has torn his prey." Even when the attribute is not expressed by a verb, but by an adjective or a substantive, there is need of a verb to give the sentence life. It is true that this verb, the verb "to lie," does not express action; but it is only because we have come by force of abstraction to deprive it of all special sense. This is evident in French and in the other Romance languages, where certain forms of the substantive verb are derived from the Latin verb *stare*.[5] Finally, in spite of our abstractions, the peculiar characteristic of the sensible action must always be attached to all our verbs and to all our propositions; it is the characteristic of time. "Hope implies desire." "Possession gives real enjoyment." Pascal. These propositions are true of all time; nevertheless they must of necessity be enunciated in the present. Syntax makes us see hope and possession as acting, desire and enjoyment as acted upon. Nothing, however, was further from the thoughts of the philosopher than these relations borrowed from the material world. It is because he has been obliged to use the scheme established by usage for the sentence; in other words, to subject himself to the law of syntax. This law constrains us to clothe our thoughts not in a metaphysical garb, but in one essentially dramatic. The being that acts, the action, the being that receives the impulse of the action, that which is affected by it in the most indirect manner, time, place of action, etc.,—these are the parts and elements of the syntactic drama. The grammatical relations are the only relations that exist between the immutable personages of this drama.

When it happens that the order of the thought is not the same with the order of the dramatic forms that are assigned to it, then it is that the order of words agrees with the thought itself and not with the form that the thought may have taken; which is certainly most natural and logical. But could this case occur? could these two movements be different from each other? Doubtless they could, since the form is not obligatory. The same thought may be expressed in different syntactic constructions, so that the ideas which concur to form the thought have sometimes one part, sometimes another, in the drama of the sentence. In spite of this change of parts, ideas do not change places in the march of thought. Consequently the words which express these ideas ought not to change places in the order of the sentence. Let us illustrate our meaning by examples. Livy, in the thirty-fourth chapter of the first Book of his History, speaks of Demaratus and his two sons Lucumo and Arruns. He relates first the history of Demaratus and Arruns, and then continues, *Lucumoni contra. omnium heredi bonorum cum divitiae jam animos facerent, auxit ducta in matrimonium Tanaquil*, etc. Observe the cast of this phrase. *Tanaquil* is the subject; it is from her that the action expressed by *auxit* proceeds. She therefore occupies the first place in the march of the syntactic drama. Yet the author has given to her the last place in the order of words. He begins his sentence with *Lucumoni*, and he has done well, for Lucumo occupies the first place in the march of his thought. Change now the grammatical *rôle* of Lucumo, as you wish; put it in the nom., gen., acc., or abl., — it matters little provided it be by this idea that you enter the subject-matter of the sentence. You can say, *Lucumo in majores spes adductus est matrimonio Tanaquilis*, or *Lucumonem in majores spes erexit ducta in matrimonium Tanaquil*. But if, while preserving the relations of syntax you wish to change the order of words, *Tanaquil auxit animos Lucumoni*, you perplex the reader by substituting an order of words contrary to the order of ideas. Albeit in the example given one can with some difficulty comprehend your meaning. But take some verses from Horace of which the sense would be entirely destroyed by a like transposition. *Nihil est ab omni parte beatum; abstulit clarum cita mors Achillem, longa Tithonum minuit senectus.* (Carm. II, 16, 30.) We shall not touch upon the relations of syntax; we shall only change the order of words by making what is called construction. (*Nihil est ab omni parte beatum*), *mors cita abstulit Achillem clarum, senectus longa minuit Tithonum.* One no longer gets the connection of ideas. It is not then arbitrarily, nor forced by the difficulties of the metre, that Horace has separated the adjectives *clarum* and *longa* from the substantives to which they belong, since the thought is obscured the moment you put them together.

So then, in translating from one language to another, if it is not possible to imitate at the same time the syntax of the original and the order of the words, retain the order of the words and disregard the grammatical relations. The passage from Horace is proof of this. "There is no perfect happiness. A premature death carried off illustrious Achilles; a long old age wore out Tithonus." Here we have a translation which seems to be entirely faithful, but which nevertheless does not render the sense of the original. Let us abandon this specious fidelity, and let us follow as near as may be possible the order of ideas and words we find in the Latin. "There is no perfect happiness. In the height of his glory a premature death snatched away Achilles; in the bosom of an eternal life Tithonus was worn out with old age." *Il n'y a pas de bonheur parfait. Une mort précoce enleva l'illustre Achille; une longue vieillesse consuma Tithon.* In order to translate the sentence from Livy we must seek to give a force to the expression which will allow us to assign the first place to Lucumo in the order of words. We shall then make it (the word Lucumo) the subject of the proposition; that is, we shall put it in the nominative, though in Latin it is in the dative. The great secret of a good translation is to find forms of expression which will allow the translator to adopt into a foreign idiom the order of words which is found in the original.[6]

If one intended to translate into Latin this passage from Voltaire, *Il avait un beau-père, il l'obligea de se pendre; il avait un beau-frère, il le fit étrangler* (He had a father-in-law, he forced him to hang himself; he had a brother-in-law, he caused him to be strangled), he would change the grammatical construction, but would not interfere with the order of ideas, putting, for example, *Soceram ad suspendium adegit, affinem strangulari jussit*. In Latin each member is composed of but one proposition; in French it is composed of two. This is because in the French, grammatical propriety does not permit the object to be put first. On the other hand, the concatenation of ideas demands that the object should stand first. What is to be done in this dilemma? It is impossible to violate the law of grammar, but it is equally impossible, at least for an author who has a proper appreciation of what he is saying, to reverse the order of the thought. Therefore to satisfy grammar and thought, Voltaire adopted the order above given. In Latin one gains the same end in a more direct manner without cutting the sentence in two; but by marking the opposition of the two parts of each sentence by a pause of voice (after *socerum* and after *affinem*), like that which is indicated by the comma. If it were desired to indicate this pause in a more marked manner, it would only be necessary to add a word of secondary emphasis and signification; *e.g.*, *socerum ille ad suspendium adegit*, or *socerum enim, quidem*, etc.

We are made to feel that there is a progression of thought which differs from that of syntax, because it is independent thereof, and because it remains the same amid the diverse transformations of the sentence, and even when we translate into a foreign tongue. But, it may be asked, what is that progression of thought, and upon what principle is it founded? Grammar has succeeded in making a complete analysis of the syntactical relations, and has formed them into a lucid system. Can it be that it is not possible to analyze the march of thought, to recognize and distinguish in it certain parts which are found in all sentences? Since it is a march, can we not find halting-places that may be pointed out? We propose to attempt such an analysis.

An attempt to set forth the march of ideas.

Thought being in its nature pure and simple, should from the nature of the case at the origin* of languages also have its most direct expression in a sound equally simple; that is, it ought to be expressed by a single word, one might even say by a monosyllable. But let us not take account of the number of syllables because a matter of no importance to our thesis. A single word ought to suffice for the expression of the thought so far as it relates to the present instant; and it ought to be perfectly clear and intelligible to him who hears it pronounced. (Primitive) man saw an occurrence, a change, an object that made an impression on him. He felt the need of reacting upon this impression by an intellectual act, and of communicating it at the same time to another person. He expressed this by a simple word, which though brusque was perfectly clear, because the object to which it related, which had given it birth, was present and served as a commentary, so to speak, for him who heard. We every day see children, per-

---

* That is, as soon as men began to give verbal expression to their mental concepts.

sons of uncultivated minds, all men, indeed, under the influence of sudden and profound emotion, express themselves by such exclamations, *The lightning! a shot! my father!* It is usual to explain this mode of speech by ellipses, *See the lightning that appears*, etc. This explanation is in harmony with our theory of the proposition. But as, in the times of which we are speaking, thought was not yet expressed in the forms of a complete proposition, it would be a mistake to assume the validity of this theory in the case before us. These exclamations, although we properly translate them by substantives, have a more living, a more verbal character, because they contain within themselves an entire sentence.

As long as thought and word followed each other closely or immediately, the very instant of perception, the unity of speech would correspond exactly with the unity of thought. But when the thought related to the past, or when it sprang in a less direct manner from the perception of sensible objects, the simple expression could no longer be easily comprehended by him to whom it was addressed, and the sentence had of necessity to be taken to pieces. It was in the first place necessary that this other personage, with whom it was desired to communicate, should be placed at the same point of view with the speaker; it was necessary that a word of introduction should precede the remark which it was intended to utter; it was necessary to lean on something present and known, in order to reach out to something less present, nearer, or unknown. There is then a point of departure, an initial notion which is equally present to him who speaks and to him who hears, which forms, as it were, the ground upon which the two intelligences meet; and another part of discourse which forms the statement (*l'énonciation*), properly so called. This division is found in almost all we say.

For example, the fact that Romulus founded the city of Rome, can, in languages that admit of a free construction, be stated in several different ways, preserving all the while the same syntax. Suppose that some one has related the story of the birth of Romulus and the marvellous events that attach thereto, he might add, *Idem Romulus Romam condidit.* While showing a traveller the city of Rome, we might say to him, *Hanc urbem condidit Ro-*

mulus. Speaking of the most celebrated foundings, and after mentioning the founding of Thebes by Cadmus, that of Athens by Cecrops, we might add, *Condidit Romam Romulus*.¹ The syntax is the same in the three sentences; in all three the subject is *Romulus*, the attribute *founded*, the direct object *Rome*. Nevertheless, three different things are said in the three sentences, because these elements, though remaining the same, are distributed in a different manner in the introduction and the principal part of the sentence. The point of departure, the rallying point of the interlocutors, is Romulus the first time, Rome the second, and the third time the idea of founding. And so the information that is to be imparted to another, the goal of the discourse, is different in the three forms of expression.

This distinction must be insisted on, for it forms the basis of the theory which we are trying to establish. In these three examples the fact under consideration is the same, yet things altogether distinct and different are stated to the hearer. The fact does not change; the sensible and exterior action is the same: these are the reasons why the syntax has remained the same; for the syntax, as we have seen above, is the image of a sensible fact. The progression, the relations of the thought, change: this is why the succession of the words ought to change also, for it is the image of the progression of the thought. Syntax relates to the exterior, to things; the succession of the words relates to the speaking subject, to the mind of man. There are in the proposition two different movements: an objective movement, which is expressed by syntactic relations; and a subjective movement, which is expressed by the order of the words. It may be said that the syntax is the principal thing because it inheres in the objects themselves, and because it does not vary with the points of view from moment to moment. But this is precisely the reason why we should attach the greatest importance to the succession of words. For in speech — or in spoken language — the most important thing is the instant of conception and utterance. Into this instant is compressed all the life of speech: before it, speech had no existence; after it, speech is dead. This moment makes the individuality of thought and spoken language, and the signet of this individuality is the order in which the ideas and signs are produced.

Application of the foregoing general remarks.

The most general initial notions, and therefore also the most frequently employed, are the relations of time and place. These are comprehended by every one, and are a sort of mental compartments in which the intellect easily places all that it can apprehend. Here we have the reasons why stories begin thus, "In Ephesus there was formerly," etc. *Tempore quo in homine non, ut nunc, omnia in unum consentiebant* is the beginning of the fable of Menenius Agrippa. λέγομεν ἡμεῖς οἱ Σπαρτιῆται γενέσθαι ἐν τῇ Λακεδαίμονι κατὰ τρίτην γενεὴν τὴν ἀπ᾽ ἐμέο Γλαῦκον Ἐπικύδεος παῖδα. (Herodotus, VI, 86.) (We Spartans say that there lived in L., etc.) One easily gains a starting-point by means of these general notions, just as one takes the cardinal points of the compass in an unknown country. Thus the French language (and the English), so exact in the observance of the analytic order, allows these general circumstances to occupy the place ordinarily reserved for the subject.

We read in the letters of Cicero to Atticus (II, 1), *Calendis Juniis, eunti mihi Antium et gladiatores M. Metelli cupide relinquenti, venit obviam tuus puer* (On the first of June, as I was going to Antium and leaving behind me the, etc.). This is exactly the reverse of what is generally called the logical order: the subject is put at the end; the complements of the verb are found at the beginning. This is the tower of Babel, M. de Bonald would say, the false language of the pagans; the perversity of speech reflects the perversity of men. This order of words undoubtedly sounded better to the ears of Cicero than the natural and logical order, Beauzée and other grammarians would say. But there is nothing more simple, nothing less artificial, less rhetorical, than this entirely familiar sentence. Change the order, make the construction logical, begin with *tuus puer*. Translate into French, *Ton esclave m'a rencontré*, etc. (Your slave met me). You no longer say what Cicero wished to say. If he were intending to reply to the question, "When did you meet my messenger?" he would have disposed the words in the order we have indicated. In this case meeting the messenger would have been the point of departure, the known fact; and the circumstances of time, etc., the goal of the discourse. But in the sentence from Cicero, these circumstances serve as an introduction for what we wish to come at in general; namely, meeting the slave sent by Atticus. The contrary case is presented in the opening sentence of another letter (VI, 1), *Accepi tuas litteras a. d. quintum Terminalia Laodiceae*. One can enter into the sentence by different gates, but there is nothing arbitrary in the choice that is made.

Often we are satisfied with a still more general and indefinite notion, as when we begin by, "one day," "somewhere," etc. *Olim rusticus urbanam murem mus* (Hor. Sat. II, 6, 79.)[8] The Romans were fond of beginning their stories with *Olim*. It often happens then that something which expresses the cause, motive, or means, is the point of departure from which we set out to arrive at the fact itself. *Concordia res parvae crescunt, discordia magnae dilabuntur.* But nothing hinders our sometimes setting out from a fact to reach the cause or the means. For example, *Parvae res augentur audacia, magnae prudentia conservantur*. In the former of these propositions the effects of concord and discord are the goal of the speaker; in the latter, this goal is the means which it is necessary to employ both in the beginnings and at the height of fortune. Voltaire says of a young man, "He killed himself to extricate himself from an unfortunate predicament." It is because he is treating of suicide, and because he indicates the different motives which determine men thereto. One killed himself because he could not endure his misery; another, because he was disgusted with his good fortune; and finally the one above spoken of, in order to extricate himself from an embarrassing situation. Suicide was therefore the thing known: the author adds the motive. But if he had wished to make us acquainted with the strange expedient thought of by this young man to get himself out of his embarrassment, he would have said, "In order to get out of his embarrassment, he slew himself." We perceive that the form of the expression changes nothing in the thing: the cause was expressed by a single word in the first example, in the second by a group of words. It could also be done by a partial proposition, *Quia natura mutari non potest, idcirco verae amicitiae sempiternae sunt.* (Cic. Lael. chap. 9.) (Because nature can not be changed, therefore true friendships are everlasting.) Here the whole first proposition is the initial notion of the thought. Cicero wishes to establish the fact that true friendships are everlasting. *Verae amicitiae sempiternae sunt, quia natura mutari non potest.* Here we see how the sentence is arranged when the speaker or writer wishes to mark the cause of this fact.

In general there is no syntactical part of the sentence, whatever may be its name, form, or extent, which may not have, in a given case, the initial notion of the thought. It would be useless, I think, to multiply examples of this. One case, however, deserves to be distinguished among others. It happens sometimes that we can find nothing which will prepare the hearer for that which we wish to communicate to him, and that, not wishing to enter into the matter without preparation, we begin with that which is most general, most indispensable, but also most insignificant; namely, with the idea of existence pure and simple. "There was a king." Ἔστι πόλις Ἐφύρη. I propose to tell you something that you do not yet know or that you are supposed not to know (otherwise I should not tell it); it is evident that I must lay hold on something that you already know, that I must make a beginning, be it only for form's sake.

This is the first rule for the communication of ideas. The Book of Genesis, which narrates the creation of the world, that is, the beginning of things, could not find in all the universe an initial notion to which it might attach itself, for the universe did not yet exist. How does the sacred writer proceed in this case? He takes for a beginning the idea of beginning itself; and in truth it seems impossible to take any other.

Let us come down to less lofty examples. Let us analyze the opening of the Cyropedia of Xenophon, a work written in a style of the utmost simplicity and naturalness. Only at the second chapter does the author enter upon his narrative. Let us see how he has managed the arrangement of his sentences. Πατρὸς μὲν δὴ λέγεται ὁ Κῦρος γενέσθαι Καμβύσου ... μητρὸς δὲ ὁμολογεῖται Μανδάνης γενέσθαι ... φῦναι δὲ ὁ Κῦρος λέγεται ... εἶδος μὲν κάλλιστος, ψυχὴν δὲ φιλανθρωπότατος ... ἐπαιδεύθη γε μὴν ἐν Περσῶν νόμοις. What is the beginning of all these propositions? Two genitives, two accusatives, an infinitive, a verb. This is the answer those would give who take the syntax as the basis of the order of words. But this answer would tell us nothing. On the contrary, it would involve us in greater difficulties, or it would even have us believe that the author had written at hap-hazard, without any logical principle. Let us then abandon the forms of syntax, which, as may be easily seen by this very example, are quite arbitrary, and let us hold to ideas. The author has put at the head of all these propositions two general ideas, — father, mother, natural traits, education, looks, soul. These are followed by particular ideas, — Cambyses, Mandane, etc. General ideas are the framework or outlines in which we may place any other as well as Cyrus; commonplaces well known to every one, and which, for this very reason, are capital initial notions. The point which the author wishes to reach, the real object of his communication, is special ideas, which in the case before us fill up the general outline or scheme. These ideas are announced in the second place. This natural progression, and one that is related to the original *de*composition of the thought, is followed in all these cases: the progression claimed to be logical, which requires, first the subject, then the attribute, then the complements, has been neglected. Translate this extract into English or French; you will displace the points of departure of the original, for they are the points of departure of the thought in the original, but you will make each of these points of departure the subject of a proposition. The father of Cyrus was Cambyses; his mother was Mandane, etc.

Thukydides begins his history of the Peloponnesian War — it is the 24th chap. of the first Book — as follows, Ἐπίδαμνός ἐστι πόλις ἐν δεξιᾷ ἐσπλέοντι τὸν Ἰόνιον κόλπον· προσοικοῦσι δ' αὐτὴν Ταυλάντιοι... ταύτην ἀπῴκισαν μὲν Κερκυραῖοι, οἰκιστὴς δ' ἐγένετο Φαλίος... ξυνῴκισαν δὲ καὶ τῶν Κορινθίων τινες.[9] It is easy to apply to this extract like observations with the foregoing. We will put by the side of these Greek passages the first lines of Voltaire's History of Charles XII., "Sweden and Finland constitute a kingdom having a breadth.... It extends from south to north ... under a severe climate which has almost no spring nor autumn. Winter reigns there nine months.... Summer produces.... The animals are. ... The men are...." It will be seen that it is always the same march in French (or in English) as in Greek. It is true that the French propositions begin with their subjects, and that the Greek propositions have at their head, sometimes this member of the sentence, sometimes that, but the order of ideas and words is not less the same in the two (or three) languages.

Modifications which the peculiar genius of a language may bring to the principle of the order of words.

To what may we then reduce the differences of construction which we find existing among languages whether ancient or modern? Languages have been divided into logical or analogical, into transpositive or inversive, according as they do or do not observe the order of syntactic analysis which has been established as the normal order. The majority of grammarians have given a diploma of honor to the analytical languages, the construction of which has been proclaimed as the only natural one. A minority has risen against this outrage upon the ancients, and, while rehabilitating the order of the Greek and the Latin, have felt called upon to disparage in some measure that of most modern languages. It has been assumed on both sides that there is an abyss between the two systems of construction; but it appears that the difference is not where it has been sought.

The ancient languages follow a different order from the modern languages. By advancing this proposition I do not believe that I am proposing a hypothesis, but stating a palpable fact. But additions have been made to the facts. Men have unconsciously mingled with the objective truth elements of subjective judgment. In order to confine one's self strictly to fact, this much at least may be said: in the ancient languages the relation of syntax to the order of words is different from that of the modern languages. It remains then to discover which of the two has been changed, the order of words or the syntactical arrangement of most of the sentences. But men have gone beyond the fact and fallen into an error which recalls a well-known optical illusion. Persons on board of a moving boat believe upon ocular evidence that the banks of the river are in motion; the world for a long time supposed that the motion of the sun was a fact attested by the sense of sight. The senses, however, only show us a change in the relation of places, and men mistook the body whose movement was the cause of this phenomenon. The same thing, it seems to me, has befallen the grammarians.

If we really arranged words in a different order from the ancients, it would justify the supposition that a change had taken place in the succession of ideas, in the logical processes even, which would constitute a very grave difference indeed. But there is nothing of the kind, and we observe the same order of ideas and words. Good translations attest this; and if we seem to observe a different one, it is because we choose from other points of observation the syntactic forms with which it is necessary to clothe thought. Men have been mistaken because in treating of the order of words they have taken the sentence ready made, with all its elements and all its relations carefully determined. It seems as if the arrangement of the words had been regarded as ancillary labor which was performed only after the thought had already been transformed into words. But if the order of words corresponds to the order of ideas, if this march of ideas exists in the thought itself before it has been clothed in grammatical forms, if the syntactical conformation only comes after and has merely a secondary influence upon the order of words, then it is evident that the aspect of the things is entirely changed. Here then lies, as we think, the difference between the ancient and modern languages.

The ancients in their languages followed the order of their ideas, and chose, in order to place them in a proper setting, that syntactical conformation which was the least artificial and most animated. They did not concern themselves to make the movement of ideas and the syntactical movement correspond with each other. The movement of the ideas is shown by the order of the words, the syntactical movement is expressed by terminations. This is all that any one could ask; this done, it is permissible to intersect the syntactical construction in every direction, to enter, to cross it, and to come out where one pleases.

In the modern languages we follow the order of ideas as in the ancient; this is the law of every reasonable being. The order of ideas is shown by the order of words. But this order of words serves at the same time more or less to express the syntactical relations. Our languages tend more and more to replace this double march of the sentence by a single one. The subject was originally but the point of departure of a sensible act which serves as a model for the construction of the sentence. Our languages tend to make of the subject the point of departure for the thought itself. This is the reason why our languages oblige us to choose a conformation of the sentence in which the syntactical march shall not deviate too greatly from that of the thought. What they demand, then, is not the sacrifice of the order of one's ideas to the syntax; on the contrary, they would have the syntax conform to the required order of the words; and we reverse the true relation of things by saying that the order of words is determined by the syntax. What is called *inversion* is not, in most cases, an illegitimate displacement of words; for to displace words would be to displace ideas, a mistake which a good writer would not make: but it is the employment of a different syntax, the author choosing, after the manner of the ancients, the most animated syntax, in place of that which accords in its march with the march of ideas.

> "He would call them back, and his voice affrights them;
> They run; his whole body is soon but one sore,
> With our mournful cries the plain resounded." [10]

If Racine had written in prose, he would certainly not have put, "The plain resounded with our mournful cries." This turn of the phrase, which rudely interrupts the order of ideas, would be much more daring than even the verse of tragedy. Prose would substitute for the sentence in the verse something like, "Our mournful cries resounded in the plain." It will be seen that the poet has not inverted the order of ideas and words, and that it is only by the choice of the syntax that analogical languages are distinguished from the transpositive.[11]

I have tried to show that men think and express themselves in the same order, whether they speak a modern language or use one of the ancient languages. It will be understood, and I hasten to add, that this assertion is not absolute. However rich a language may be in syntactical resources, it cannot possibly provide such a variety of forms as shall in all cases be analogous to the innumerable modifications of which the march of the thought is susceptible. These two marches or progressions cannot therefore be always in accord. In modern languages, and even in that which is so to speak the most modern of them all, the French, one may deviate, in certain cases, from the strict order of analysis. In such cases the order of ideas has gained the mastery over the syntactical order. On the other hand, the natural march of ideas is sometimes sacrificed in order to suit one's thoughts to the syntactical order. Such cases are more difficult to verify, as they are much less evident; they are also, it seems to me, much more uncommon than the others.

Nevertheless, if I am not mistaken, the style of our languages exhibits some little of this inconvenience to which a writer is put who adopts an order analogous to the syntax. Let us cite a few examples. Voltaire expresses himself as follows on the condemnation of Augustus de Thou: " All that can be said of such a sentence is that it was not passed by justice but by commissioners. The letter of the murderous law was precise. It is not alone the prerogative of lawyers but of all men to say whether the spirit of the law was not perverted. It is a sad contradiction that a few men should put to death as a criminal him whom a whole nation judges innocent and worthy of esteem." (Commentaire sur le livre des delits, etc.) The thoughts contained in these sentences fit perfectly to each other, but the sentences themselves are unconnected. Each sentence seems to have a beginning, an independent march, as if it were a stranger to the other sentences which surround it. This is because the syntactic march deviates here from that of the ideas; it is because the points of departure of each sentence are not taken as they would have been in Greek or Latin. Let us translate this piece into Greek, in order better to appreciate this difference in the style of the languages. Περὶ τοιαύτης κρίσεως (the author has just given a history of the case) τοῦτο μόνον ἂν λέγοιτο, ὅτι οὐχ οἱ κύριοι αὐτῆς ἔκριναν δικασταί, ἀλλὰ παρηλλαγμένοι τινὲς ἐπίτηδες εἰς τοῦτο λεκτοί. Τὰ μὲν ῥήματα ἀκριβῆ

ἦν τοῦ νόμου τοῦ φονίου· τὴν δὲ διάνοιαν τοῦ νόμου σκέψασθαι, εἰ οὐκ ἄρα διεστράφη, παντός ἐστιν, οὐ τῶν νομικῶν μόνων. Εἰ δ' ὑπ' ὀλίγων τινῶν θανατοῦται ὡς ἄδικος ὤν, ὃς ἀναίτιός τε καὶ πολλοῦ ἄξιος κέκριται ὑπὸ τῶν πολιτῶν ἁπάντων, πῶς οὐχὶ τοῦτό γε δεινότατον ἂν εἴη καὶ ἀλογώτατον.
"If there are two milliards in a kingdom, all the commodities and manual labor will cost double what they would cost if there were but one milliard. I am as rich with fifty thousand livres income, when I buy a pound of meat for four sous, as with a hundred thousand when I pay eight for it; and so with other things in proportion. The true wealth of a kingdom does not then consist of gold and silver: it consists in the abundance of all commodities, in work and industries. It is not long ago that there might be seen on the river La Plata a Spanish regiment, the officers of which had golden swords, but they were without shirts and bread." (Dial. d'un philos. et d'un controleur, etc.) I believe that in the ancient languages a writer would have commenced the second sentence with "fifty thousand livres income"; the third with "gold and silver"; the fourth with "golden swords." In virtue of these changes the *ensemble* of the sentences would have formed a continuous whole.

"In truth it is not gold and silver which make life comfortable — it is natural disposition. A people which should have only these metals would be very miserable; a people that without these metals should put to a happy use all the productions of the earth would be truly a rich people. France has this advantage, with a great deal more ready money than is necessary for circulation." (S. de Louis XIV. chap. 30.) If the two members of the second sentence began with the idea of *these metals*, and if the third began with *this advantage*, the discourse would be more connected, but it would not therefore be more French. Let these passages from Voltaire be compared with selections taken from ancient authors; a marked difference in the character of the composition will be evident.

Greek and Latin sentences form a chain of which the parts interlink. French sentences may be compared to a necklace of pearls; they are joined only by the thread of the thought. It is true that the articulation of connected discourse in the ancient languages is produced by several means which are foreign to the subject of this thesis, such as the employment of relatives instead of demonstratives, the various forms of attraction, the great number of conjunctive adverbs, and so on. But among these means, that which seems to hold the first place, is the fact that the succession of words, independent of syntax, retraces for us the faithful image of the succession of ideas. The old French had not yet entirely lost the happy flexibility of the Latin. Naturally and without studied effort, but with a perfect grace, Joinville writes sentences like the following: "Et si ce ne vous plet à faire, si le faites aquiter du tréu que il doit à l'Ospital et au Temple, et il se tendra à paié de vous. Au Temple et à l'Ospital il rendoit lors tréu pour ce que," etc. (Chap. LXXXIX). (If this does not please you to do, if you will cause him to be acquitted of the troth that he owes, etc.)

Translations, even the most faithful, lend credibility to this difference in the genius of languages, for, though following closely the Greek and the Latin, they have not ceased to be French. I select a passage translated by M. Cousin from Plato: "Je dis donc qu'il y a dans le corps et l'âme je ne sais quoi qui fait juger qu'ils sont l'un et l'autre en bon état, quoi qu'ils ne s'en portent pas mieux pour cela. Voyons si je ne pourrai faire entendre plus clairement ce que je veux. Je dis qu'il y a deux arts qui se rapportent au corps et à l'âme."

Δυοῖν ὄντοιν τοῖν πραγμάτοιν δύο λέγω τέχνας.[12] The Greek takes its point of departure in the two things, the body and the soul, which have just been spoken of; thence it leads us to the two arts, the new ideas, which are the goal of the sentence, "Celui qui répond à l'âme j'appelle politique. Pour l'autre qui regarde le corps, je ne saurais le désigner d'abord par un seul nom. Mais, quoique la culture du corps soit une, j'en faits deux parties, dont l'une est la gymnastique et l'autre la médecine. En divisant de même la politique en deux, je mets la puissance législative, vis-à-vis de la gymnastique, et la puissance judiciaire vis-à-vis de la médecine." ἀντίστροφον μὲν τῇ γυμναστικῇ τὴν νομοθετικήν, ἀντίστροφον δὲ τῇ ἰατρικῇ τὴν δικαιοσύνην. In the Greek the dative twice precedes the accusative, because gymnastics and medicine are known. "Elle (la flatterie) ne se met nullement en peine du bien; mais par l'appât du plaisir elle attire la folie et s'en fait adorer. La cuisine s'est glissée sous la médecine." ὑπὸ μὲν οὖν τὴν ἰατρικὴν ἡ ὀψοποτικὴ ὑποδέδυκε. (Gorgias 464.)

Cookery is the subject of the sentence, and for this reason stands first in French. But it is the new idea which the author wishes to introduce to us, and which stands in relation to medicine, a thing already known. This is the reason why medicine is expressed in Greek before cookery. I will not pursue this investigation further. The more excellent a translation is and the more accurately it brings out the delicate shades of meaning of the original, the more we are inclined to believe that the divergences belong to the very genius of the two languages. There is nothing more easy and more simple than the turns of expression so frequent in Homer, Τὸν δ᾽ ἀπαμειβόμενος προσέφη πόδας ὠκὺς Ἀχιλλεύς. This verse, simple as it is, could not well be rendered into modern French. "Achille aux pieds légers lui repondit" (Achilles with nimble feet to him replied) is very abrupt, very disconnected. Homer is making the transition from the speaker whom we have just heard to him whom we are about to hear. In the translation we find the latter upon the stage without knowing how he got there. Joinville was still free to say (Chap. LXXX): "A ceulz parla le roy en tel manière" (To them spoke the king in this wise). In place of regarding the syntactic march, he follows the march of the thought. In the case above cited he has just named the lords that constitute the council of Saint Louis.

These transitions of thought which are so perfectly rendered in the ancient languages may be infinitely varied; nor is it possible to reduce them to a system.[13] We believe, however, that there are two types so distinctly marked that they may be indicated with precision. If the initial notion is related to the united notion of the preceding sentence, the march of the two sentences is to some extent parallel; if it is related to the goal of the sentence which precedes, there is a progression in the march of the discourse. *Edito imperio signum secutum est. Jussa miles exsequitur. Clamor hostes circumsonat. Superat deinde castra hostium et in castra consulis pervenit.* (Livy III, 28.)

Here we have a progression from one sentence to the next.

The goal of the first sentence is the signal given. This is the point of departure of the second, *Jussa*. The point of departure of the third, *clamor*, is an expression varied from the goal of the second, *miles exsequitur*. In the third the cry has reached the besiegers; in the fourth we see it continue its progress till it reaches the besieged. These are the parts of the chain that interlink, — if I may be allowed to designate by this figure what bears an individual character in this march of the discourse. Thus far there has been progression, but setting out from this point we shall have some parallel links. *Alibi pavorem, alibi gaudium ingens facit. Romani, civilem esse clamorem atque auxilium adesse inter se gratulantes, ultro ex stationibus ac vigiliis territant hostem. Consul differendum negat.* The *alibi* of the second phrase refers back to the *alibi* of the first with which it is contrasted. *Romani* of the third is the same thing as the second *alibi*. *Consul* of the fourth is opposed to *Romani* of the third. We have here then in every case points of departure that are related to points of departure of the preceding sentences, and this constitutes what I have called the parallel march of the sentences. Whether the march be progressive or parallel the relation to what precedes is, as may be seen, either that of equality or of opposition. Nevertheless the relation of equality is more closely related to the progressive march, the relation of opposition to the parallel march.

In the example from Livy, the progressive or parallel form of the sentences corresponds to the progressive or parallel form of the facts; and it is in this accordance between the objects of the recital and its form that the greatest charm of this passage consists. Yet these relations of sentences do not belong exclusively to narrative; a purely intellectual development may also furnish them. *Quod semper movetur, aeternum est. Quod autem motum affert alicui, quodque ipsum agitatur aliunde, quando finem habet motus, vivendi finem habeat necesse est. Solum igitur quod seipsum movet, quia nunquam deseritur a se, nunquam ne moveri quidem desinit. Quin etiam ceteris quae moventur hic fons, hoc principium est movendi. Principii autem nulla est origo. Nam ex principio oriuntur omnia: ipsum autem nulla ex re alia nasci potest.*[14] (Cic. Tusc. I, 23–4.) Once only does the initial notion of a sentence support itself upon the goal of the preceding. This is in the proposition which begins with *Principii autem*. Here we have then a progressive march. In the others the march is parallel, and in a large majority the connection is made by means of a relation of opposition.

By an artifice which is very familiar to ancient authors, the progressive march is employed in place of the parallel march in the rhetorical figure called chiasmus, which consists in a cross arrangement of the symmetrical parts of the discourse. *Audires ululatus feminarum, infantium quiritatus, clamores virorum,* says Pliny, Ep. VI. Βασιλεὺς γὰρ καὶ τύραννος ἅπαν ἐχθρὸς ἐλευθερία καὶ νόμοις ἐναντίοις (Demos. Phil. II).[15] (For every king and every absolute monarch is the opponent of liberty and the enemy of laws.)

The pathetic order.

The two elements of the sentence which we have named the initial notion and the goal, do not always follow each other in the order in which we have considered them here. There are two conditions under which they follow each other in the reverse order from that indicated above, and there are other cases in which the initial notion is wholly wanting. We claim that in the movement from the initial notion to the goal had in view, we have revealed the movement of the human mind itself. It may cause surprise, perhaps, that we should be willing to admit the reversal of this march or movement lest we should also overturn our whole theory at the same time. We shall return to this objection farther on. For the present let us begin with an example. In the Persae (v. 181 ff.) of Aeschylus, Atossa narrates her dream in these words, —

> Ἐδοξάτην μοι δύο γυναῖκ' εὐείμονε,
> Ἡ μὲν πέπλοισι Περσικοῖς ἠσκεμένη,
> Ἡ δ' αὖτε Δωρικοῖσιν, εἰς ὄψιν μολεῖν.

(There seemed to come into my view two women richly clad, the one in Persian robes, the other in Dorian.) She had reported a vision, she therefore begins very properly with the verb Ἐδοξάτην; next come the object of this vision, δύο γυναῖκε, then the details.

Μεγέθει τε τῶν νῦν ἐκπρεπέστατα πολὺ
Κάλλει τ' ἀμώμῳ, καὶ κασιγνήτα γένους
Ταὐτοῦ· πάτραν δ' ἔναιον, ἡ μὲν Ἑλλάδα
Κλήρῳ λαχοῦσα γαῖαν, ἡ δὲ βάρβαρον.

(In stature they were taller than are the women of our day; in beauty faultless, and sisters of the same race. But they dwelt in different countries, the land of Greece had fallen to the lot of one; a foreign to the other.)

The reader will notice in these sentences the march that we have called attention to, above. At first we have general schemes or outlines which are then filled up with special ideas. In the verses which follow, the queen narrates the quarrel of the two women, the attempt of Xerxes to fasten them to his chariot, the difference in the way they bore the yoke, the one with joy and pride, the other with aversion at the insult. The march of all these sentences is like the march of those which precede. Then Atossa continues πίπτει δ' ἐμὸς παῖς. The real goal of this sentence is evidently the fall, πίπτει. Ἐμὸς παῖς is added because one of two women is spoken of in the preceding sentence. These two words would then have been a very appropriate *point of departure*. It will be seen that the order of the two elements of the sentence is reversed. This takes place because Atossa is carried away by her emotion. Thus far her narrative had been orderly and deliberate, but having reached its crisis she is no longer able to follow the thread of her recital; she sees only the fall, and this word escapes her lips in spite of herself. It is not till afterward that she becomes aware of the gap in her account, when she traverses again that part of the way over which she had before passed with unbecoming haste.

In the Antigone of Sophocles, the messenger who relates the sad end of Antigone and Haemon, having reported that Kreon and his suite were coming toward the tomb, continues in these words, φωνῆς δ' ἄπωθεν ὀρθίων κωκυμάτων Κλύει τις ἀκτέριστον ἀμφὶ παστάδα. (Antig. 1206–7.) (And some one hears from afar the voice of loud lament in the vicinity of that unconsecrated chamber.) The continuity of the discourse would have required that he should first designate the place whence the voice came; for this place is known, having just been spoken of. But startled as he has been by these sudden misfortunes, he consoles himself at first by expressing the thought that is the goal of the sentence after which comes the one that is its point of departure. The peculiar effect of this order will be better seen upon comparing it with a passage of Electra, analogous as to matter but different in the turn of expression. It is Chrysothemis who is speaking,

> Ἐπεὶ γὰρ ἦλθον πατρὸς ἀρχαῖον τάφον,
> Ὁρῶ κολώνης ἐξ ἄκρας νεορρύτους
> Πηγὰς γάλακτος ... ἐσχάτης δ' ὁρῶ
> Πυρᾶς νεωρῆ βόστρυχον τετμημένον.

(For as I was drawing near the ancient tomb of my father I saw from the summit of the hillock fresh libations of milk ... and I saw on the highest part of the mound a freshly-cut lock of hair.) In this case the narrative advances step by step.

These examples are sufficient to show the character of the inverted order and the state of the soul whose natural expression it is. When the imagination is vividly impressed, or when the sensibilities of the soul are deeply stirred, the speaker enters into the matter of his discourse at the goal, and we do not become aware, till afterward, of the successive steps by which he could have entered had his mind been in a more tranquil state. It is in the poets chiefly, but sometimes in the orators, that these tropes are found. *In medias res auditorem rapiunt.* It is their characteristic in the composition of a story as well as in the details of diction.

Our modern languages, as we have seen, are sometimes hampered by considerations of syntax when they are called upon to represent the regular advance of the ancient languages; it is equally the case when we attempt to imitate the pathetic march. This constraint may have a double effect; we may either refrain entirely from expressing the emotions of the soul by the arrangement of our words, or we may express them in a much more violent manner than in the free languages,

> Τῶν ἐν Θερμοπύλαις θανόντων
> Εὐκλεὴς μὲν ἁ τύχα, καλὸς δ' ὁ πότμος,
> Βωμὸς δ' ὁ τάφος, πρὸ γόων δὲ μνᾶστις, ὁ δ' οἶκτος ἔπαινος.

(Glorious is their lot, beautiful their end, an altar their tomb, for tears they have remembrance, for mourning, praises.) Βωμὸς δ' ὁ τάφος may be translated either, "their tomb is an altar," but then we do not translate the animation expressed in the succession of words; or "an altar is their tomb," and we translate it with more force than the Greek. In the latter version the idea made prominent is detached from the other idea to which it is joined; a little proposition apart is made of it. The emotion of the soul shows itself despite the reflective character of the language used; and it shows itself more violently because it has an obstacle to overcome.

It is hardly necessary to add that the inverted order of which we have just spoken is very distinct from what is ordinarily called inversion. Everything is called inversion which is a departure from the analytic and syntactic order. We have given examples which violate the syntactical order and do not follow this order from the point of departure to the goal of the sentence. On the other hand it may happen that the syntactic order is observed, and that the goal of the sentence is announced before the initial notion. A single chapter from Livy will furnish several examples. Tarquin crying out, *Ferrum in manu est*, Lucretia saying, *Vestigia viri alieni in lecto sunt tuo*, belong here. *Ceterum corpus tantum violatum est, animus insons, mors testis erit* are expressed almost in the analytic order; nevertheless they deviate from the tranquil and orderly march, which, while observing the legitimate order, would have reversed the analytic order. *In manu ferrum est. In lecto tuo, Collatine, vestigia sunt viri alieni. Testis erit mors.* (Bk. I, 58.)

Let us return now to the objection indicated above. To put first an order conformable to the march of the thought itself, and next to admit that we may, though expressing ourselves perfectly well, speak in the inverted order, — is not this to tear down what we have ourselves just built up? I do not think that we need be surprised at these apparent contradictions, but that we must recognize the fact that language follows sometimes one principle, sometimes another.

There is nothing in nature which may not be drawn in different directions by different influences in turn. The mind of man is subject to the same law. Why then should not languages which are the image of the human mind be subject to it? It is evident, on the contrary, that a language will be perfect in proportion as it is a faithful reflector of these varying states, a plastic wax capable of receiving the impression of every inequality, every undulation of the human mind. The Greek is recognized as being one of the most perfect languages that has ever existed. However paradoxical it may appear I find the perfection of this language to lie largely in the absence of every exclusive or unconditional rule. Take a Greek grammar and examine the chapter on the correspondence of the tenses, modes, hypothetical propositions, or any other, and you will find everywhere that one is allowed to make all possible combinations. The grammar does not give the inexorable law; it allows the mind complete liberty to choose what can best express all the delicate shades of its thought. Our languages to a limited extent impose laws on the human mind. The Greek receives it; one can make a very greatly varied use of it, one can also more easily abuse it. But in our languages the order of the words is of all parts of the grammar that which yields most easily to the momentary impulses of the mind. It is no contradiction then to admit two opposite marches of this order, if the mind itself varies in its march. The axiom which we have placed at the beginning of this chapter is that the order of words should correspond to the order of ideas. In order then to correspond to it, if the latter changes or is reversed, the former must also change or reverse its movement.

---

[1] Compare notes [2] and [3] on p. 112.

[2] It is unfortunate that this very serviceable term is not more generally used in our English grammars. As it may designate any word that modifies, qualifies or limits another word, I have sometimes simply transferred it untranslated.

[3] The old French form of the accusative case was different from the nominative. We find sentences like the following: "Moult de chevaliers et d'autres gens tenoient li Sarrazin pris en une court." Joinville. W.

[4] This statement is doubtless too strong. That the great majority of roots in the primitive language or languages had a verbal nature is not disputed, but that some were purely demonstrative is equally certain; at least there is no evidence as yet accessible that points to any probability

that these two classes can ever be reduced to one. By roots as here used we mean the elements of speech which existed before the development of the means of grammatical distinction. Their prime characteristic is that they are or were monosyllabic; nor must the terms verbal and demonstrative when applied to them be understood in strict literalness. Take, for example, the radical element *duc;* add to it the suffix *s*, the remnant of another root, and we get *dux*, meaning 'leader'; annex *o*, and we get *duco*, 'I lead'; add *tio* or *tus*, and we get 'leading,' and so on. The longer words are formed by combining several roots. It is held by many philologists that there is nothing in a root which makes it possible to determine whether the noun-element or the verb-element predominates. See also Allen & Greenough's Latin Gram. Index, under Roots.

⁵ The present tense of the French verb 'to be' in all its forms is simply a corruption of the corresponding Latin forms. They are

LATIN	OLD FRENCH	MOD. FRENCH
sum	suys, seu	suis
es	es, ies,	es
est	est	est
sumus	somes	sommes
estis	estes, iestes	etes
sunt	sont	sont

The imperfect, however, seems to be derived from the same tense of the verb 'stare.' The forms are

LATIN	OLD FRENCH	MOD. FRENCH
stabam	estoie	étais
stabas	estoies	étais
stabat	estoit	était
stabamus	estiens (ons)	étions
stabatis	estieiz	étiez
stabant	estoient	étaient

It may surprise us a little to discover this lack of homogeneity; yet, owing to the colorless nature of the verb expressing simple existence, there are in all languages several verbs that may perform its duties equally well. Two or more of these are frequently fitted together, so that what is lacking in one is supplied by the other. Of this the verbs given above are an example. In Latin the verb 'to be' has two roots, found in *esse* and *fui;* in English it has three, found in *am, was,* and *been* respectively. Simple existence may be, and is, expressed in several ways, all of the words so used, however, expressing physical acts. 'As,' the root from which the Latin 'es' and the English 'a-mi' are derived, meant originally either 'to breathe' or 'to sit'; so ϕv meant 'to grow.' Change in existence is also expressed by several words even in English: "He went mad," "he became sick," "he grew excited," etc.

⁶ Translations can be most accurately and elegantly made between languages that have the most characteristics in common. It is easier to make a relatively faithful translation from Greek or Latin into German, among modern languages, than into English or French. Again, there is a closer resemblance between Greek and German than between Greek and Latin; for while these languages are both considerably inflected,— the latter more than the former, — the German, besides possessing a good degree of inflection, readily admits the formation of compounds, and the powers of the Latin in this respect are but limited. Voss's translation of Homer may perhaps be considered as the most successful translation of an ancient poetic author into a modern language that has ever been made.

Professor Jowett's prose translations from the Greek are held in high repute, but those who insist on a good degree of literalness find fault with them. Taylor's translation of Faust, and Longfellow's of the Divina Commedia, though not from ancient languages, approach pretty closely to what would seem to be Professor Weil's ideal in this respect. Two American translations of Homer, that of Munford and that of Bryant, possess a high degree of merit.

[7] Let the English reader take some familiar passage, for example, "The fear of the Lord is the beginning of wisdom," and let him read it first with the emphasis on *fear*, then on *Lord*, next on *beginning*, and next on *wisdom*. He will get a different meaning each time. The same effects were produced in the ancient languages, and likewise in the more extensively inflected modern languages, by position.

[8] In this verse the arrangement is singularly felicitous. After introducing two persons, one a resident of the country, the other of the city, *rusticus urbanum*, Horace adds by way of explanation that they were two mice *murem mus*, and expects the reader "to see the point" at a glance.

[9] Professor Jowett translates this extract as follows: "The city of Epidamnus is situated on the right hand as you sail up the Ionic Gulf. Near it dwell the Taulantians . . . The place was colonized by the Corcyreans, but under the leadership of a Corinthian, Phalias, son of Eratokleides . . . and Corinthians also joined the colony."

[10] Racine's words are, —

Il veut les rappeler, et sa voix les effraie;
Ils courent : tout son corps n'est bientôt
   qu'une plaie,
De nos cris douloureux la plaine retentit.

[11] On comparing the phraseology of the French [or English] and Latin, we come upon many facts which corroborate the statement of the text. *Mihi est liber, mihi est nomen Carolo*, j'ai un livre [I have a book], j'ai, je porte le nom de Charles [my name is Charles, I bear the name Charles]. Δαρείου καὶ Παρυσάτιδος γίγνονται παῖδες δύο, Darius et Parysatis eurent deux fils [Dar. and Par. had two sons]. *Mihi scribendum est*, je dois écrire, il faut que j'écrire [I must write]. We change the syntax to get the two forward movements into agreement, but the ancients were not disagreeably affected by their incongruity. Among the means of bringing about this agreement, the use of the passive deserves particular attention. I subjoin the judicious remarks of M. de Sacy in reference to this point : " We sometimes employ the passive when we wish to fix the attention of those to whom we are speaking on the person or thing which is the object of the action rather than on the acting subject. Then the subject is expressed merely as a part or circumstance of the action by means of a preposition of which it becomes the object. When I am relating the history of Britannicus, I end by saying, Brit. was poisoned at the table of Nero by Nero himself. If, on the other hand, my object was to expose in detail the crimes of Nero, I should say, Nero poisoned Britannicus at his table, because I am less concerned about making known the death of Britannicus than the crime of Nero. This use of the passive is especially frequent in languages having a fixed construction and admitting but few inversions." *Principes de Grammaire générale* 3ᵉ édit., p. 161. Becker (p. 20 of the second vol. of his German Grammar)

is in agreement with the learned Frenchman on this point. W.

The use of the passive is much more extensive in English than in French, or in fact than in any language ancient or modern. See Mätzner's Eng. Grammatik, 3te Aufl. I, p. 344, and elsewhere.

[12] I have left the original in the text, and give the Greek of Plato with the translation of Professor Jowett in the notes: Τὸ τοιοῦτον λέγω καὶ ἐν σώματι εἶναι καὶ ἐν ψυχῇ, ὅ τι ποιεῖ μὲν δοκεῖν εὖ ἔχειν τὸ σῶμα καὶ τὴν ψυχήν, ἔχει δ' οὐδὲν μᾶλλον. Φέρε δή σοι, ἐὰν δύνωμαι, σαφέστερον ἐπιδείξω ὃ λέγω, δυοῖν ὄντοιν τοῖν πραγμάτοιν δύο λέγω τέχνας· τὴν μὲν ἐπὶ τῇ ψυχῇ πολιτικὴν καλῶ, τὴν δὲ ἐπὶ σώματι μίαν μὲν οὕτως ὀνομάσαι οὐκ ἔχω σοι, μιᾶς δὲ οὔσης τῆς τοῦ σώματος θεραπείας δύο μόρια λέγω, τὴν μὲν γυμναστικήν, τὴν δὲ ἰατρικήν· τῆς δὲ πολιτικῆς ἀντὶ μὲν τῆς γυμναστικῆς τὴν νομοθετικήν, ἀντίστροφον δὲ τῇ ἰατρικῇ τὴν δικαιοσύνην ... καὶ τοῦ μὲν βέλτιστον οὐδὲν φροντίζει, τῷ δὲ ἀεὶ ἡδίστῳ θηρεύεται τὴν ἄνοιαν καὶ ἐξαπατᾷ, ὥστε δοκεῖ πλείστου ἀξία εἶναι, ὑπὸ μὲν οὖν τὴν ἰατρικὴν ἡ ὀψοποιικὴ ὑποδέδυκε, ... (Gorgias, 464 B, Chap. XX).

"And this applies not only to the body, but also to the soul; in either there may be that which gives the appearance of health and not the reality. And now I will endeavor to explain to you more clearly what I mean: the soul and the body being two, have two arts corresponding to them. There is the art of politics attending on the soul, and another art attending on the body, of which I know no specific name, but which may be described as having two divisions, one of which is gymnastic, and the other medicine. And in politics there is a legislative part, which answers to gymnastic, as justice does to medicine ... and has no regard for men's highest interests, but is ever making pleasure the bait of the unwary, and deceiving them into the belief that she is of the highest value to them. Cookery simulates the disguise of medicine."

[13] It is perhaps not without interest to examine in each particular case the propriety of the transition: "I was going down yesterday to the Peiraeus with Glauco, the son of Aristo, to witness the festival" ... "Afterward, we returned to the city." Nearly thus does Plato begin his dialogue Politeia. Then he goes on, κατιδὼν οὖν πόρρωθεν ἡμᾶς οἴκαδε ὡρμημένους Πολέμαρχος ὁ Κεφάλου ἐκέλευσε, etc. We are struck with the position of the initial participle, but nothing could be more natural. S. and G. enter the Peiraeus on the day of the festival. It stands to reason that they were noticed by many persons. The idea or notion of noticing makes the starting point of the sentence. But who is this that has observed them and upon whom the author directs our attention? The name of Pol. ought properly to come next. The beginning of Xenophon's Hellenics shows us an analogous tiansition. Doricus arrives with forty vessels: κατιδὼν δὲ ὁ Ἀθηναίων ἡμεροσκόπος ἐσήμηνε τοῖς στρατηγοῖς. We may, if we wish, find plenty of similar passages, though it will hardly be possible to classify all the instances that we may meet with. W.

[14] "That which is always moved is eternal; but that which gives motion to something else, and is moved itself by some external cause, when that motion ceases, must necessarily cease to exist. That, therefore, alone, which is self-moved, because it is never forsaken by itself, can never cease to be moved. Besides, it is the beginning

and principle of motion to everything else; but whatever is a principle has no beginning, for all things arise from that principle, and it cannot itself owe its rise to anything else" (Yonge).

[15] Compare Luke xvi, 3. "I cannot dig; to beg I am ashamed." Many examples of this construction may be readily found in Xenophon's Anabasis.

CHAPTER II.

THE RELATION BETWEEN THE ORDER OF WORDS AND THE
SYNTACTICAL FORM OF THE PROPOSITION.

Classification of languages in respect to construction.

WE have tried in the preceding chapter to trace back the order of words to the order of ideas considered apart from the syntax. Nevertheless in many languages, if not in a majority, the syntax and the order of the parts of the proposition move forward abreast, mutually influencing each other. It is of this mutual relation between the syntactical interlacement and the succession of words, that is, of construction properly so-called, that the second chapter will treat. In the first chapter the general principle was under discussion; in the second we shall consider its application to particular languages.

A general classification of languages in respect to construction has long been made. Abbé Girard was the first, I believe, to establish the distinction of analogous or analytical and transpositive or inversive languages. May I be permitted, while adopting this classification, to make it more general? The idea of analogous languages is based upon the usage of the Romance languages, and primarily upon the French. But there are other languages the construction of which is in most cases closely bound up with the syntactical relation of the parts of the proposition, without being parallel to the analytical progression like the French construction. These languages will of necessity come under the first class. In languages of the second class the syntax does not make the law for the arrangement of the sentence; these languages are then only inversive from our point of view; strictly speaking, we ought not to consider them with reference to the question of inversion, for where there is no law there is no transgression of a law. Our languages might perhaps more properly be called inversive, for the very reason that they are analogous. Let us change, then, a little the idea and the names of these two classes when we distinguish them, and let us speak of languages with a free construction and languages with a fixed construction.

Free construction is a matter of privilege in inflected languages. It is evident that the arrangement of the sentence can be independent of the syntax only so far as the grammatical relations of words are clearly indicated by sonorous and varied terminations. If the inflections are lacking, or if the syntactical relations are indicated by means of affixes or of prepositions, it is inadmissible to separate those words which form a syntactical group. The order of these groups themselves may be varied without inconvenience, yet the genius of these languages, which is nothing more than established usage, often keeps this freedom within narrower bounds than clearness would demand. Certain languages too are without inflections or affixes, and even, to a certain extent, without syntactic particles. The office of these words in the sentence, their connection and their mutual dependence, are wholly or almost wholly determined by the order in which they follow each other. This order is almost or quite invariable. Between absolute invariableness and absolute inflexibility there are degrees. We say that the construction of a language is fixed, or that it is free, according as it approaches most nearly one or the other of these extremes.

If there are any languages which allow a free construction Greek and Latin belong undoubtedly to this class. It is true that the Latins were fond of placing the verb after its complements. It is true also that there are in Latin a large number of ready-coined phrases which put the adjective after its substitute, such as *populus Romanus, res publica, vir bonus*. But one would not found upon this fact a system of usual construction the rules of which would be contradicted a hundred times on any page of every Latin author. This is still more largely true of the Greek.

I do not wish to disguise the fact that the compiler of an excellent grammar has formulated the rule that the normal construction in Greek requires the attribute to be preceded by its complements, and the subject, as well as every substantive, to be followed by it.

Every other arrangement of the sentence he regards an inversion. To Kühner belongs the merit of being the first to treat in a special chapter, of the order of words in Greek; but the general rule that he has placed at the head of the chapter is constantly violated on his own admission, by Greek authors. He would appear therefore to have set up the rule merely to conform to the practice of our grammars, and under the influence of the systematizing spirit which seeks to reduce syntax to a regular scheme. Few would refuse, I think, to class Greek and Latin among the languages with a free construction. If we examine these languages the construction of which obeys either an immutable law or a usage more or less strict, we shall very soon distinguish a certain number of diverse methods easy to grasp and to characterize.[1]

In French as in the other Romance languages the fundamental rule of construction requires the subject to be placed first, then the complements (or modifiers) of the subject, next the verb, and last the complements of the verb. Stating the case in general terms we may say that the dependent word is placed after that which governs it.

The German, as well as all the languages of the same stock, agrees with the French in an important particular. It requires that in all principal sentences the verb should be put in the midst of the sentence before the attribute and after the subject or that part of the proposition which occupies its place. We say therefore *Gott schuf die Welt* in the same order that we say in French *Dieu créa le monde* (God created the world). But the complements, whether of the subject or of the attribute, are generally placed before the terms which they modify. The adjective is followed by its substantive and preceded by its complements. If the verb is in a compound tense, it is only the auxiliary that is put in the middle of the sentence, the attributive part of the verb is put at the end, after the complements. Of these complements that which belongs most closely to the attributive part of the verb, usually the direct complement (or object), is placed last after the indirect complement (or object), which in its turn is preceded by words or phrases expressing circumstance. Accordingly a German says, *Eine ploetzliche Freude hat diesem Unglueclichen das Leben gekostet* (A sudden joy has to this unfortunate (person) the life cost). *Von der mitwelt verkannte Dichter erwarten von der Nachwelt ein gerechteres Urtheil.* (Literally, By contemporaries unappreciated poets await from posterity a more just judgment.) In subordinate sentences the verb, attributive as well as auxiliary, is always placed at the end. *Man weiss dass Rom den unterworfenen voelkern seine Sprache aufzwang.* (Literally, One knows that Rome on the subject peoples its language imposed.)[2]

English has adopted the French order for the complements of the verb, but it has held to the German usage by placing the governing substantive after the adjectives belonging to it and after the substantives governed by it without the aid of a preposition. The king's eldest son has given a feast to the citizens. *Le fils ainé du roi a donné une fête aux citoyens. Des Koenig's aeltester Sohn hat den Buergern ein Fest gegeben.*

Will it be allowed to place by the side of these languages an idiom so different from ours that the terminology employed in our grammars can only be applied thereto by a sort of abuse of language? The Chinese, a language composed of invariable monosyllables, does not distinguish the parts of speech by any outward sign: neither the verb, nor the noun, nor the particles, nor any word has received a form peculiar to itself, nor does it bear any characteristic stamp. Yet the construction of the Chinese sentence is perfect; and it is a curious fact that this construction has some affinity with the English. In Chinese, qualificative epithets are placed before the name of the thing to which they belong; the subject is placed before the attribute; the direct complement is placed after the attribute and is followed by the indirect complement. Adverbial phrases, simple or compound, modifying or circumstantial, generally precede the word which they qualify. For example, *Coeli filius potest designare virum ad coelum.* (The emperor may present to heaven a man to succeed him.)[3]

As we have now passed outside the pale of European languages, let us notice a type of construction, to wit, that offered by the Turkish and by all the idioms of the Tartar family in general, such as the Mandtchu, the Mongol, and others. In these languages the adjective is always placed before its substantive, the governed substantive before the governing substantive, the complement before the verb; instead of prepositions they have postpositions, the subordinate proposition precedes the principal.[4] "The horses of the pasha's son," will be in Turkish, *Padissae filii equi*. (Literally, The pasha's son's horses.) "He is going to light a candle." *Lucernam ascensum it.* "We have seen that one finds consolation in many ills in devout prayers." *Piis precibus in multorum malorum solatia inveniri vidimus.* "The yellow stars called the gate of the general of the army come after the constellation Oudirabhalkouni." *Exercitus ducis porta vocatae flavae stellae Udir, stellas post veniunt.* What is chiefly remarkable is that the order of construction in these languages is not, as is the case in the Romance languages, a usual order which may be modified in cases more or less frequent but that it is fixed and immovable. Yet several of these languages have a varied system of suffixes which enable them to express with much precision all the relations of the syntax of dependence. It is true the syntax of agreement is less perfectly expressed. The place of each word is invariably fixed in each sentence and all sentences are as it were cast in the same mould. The governing word is always placed after the governed, and the principal verb, to which are related directly or indirectly all the words of a sentence, should always be put at the end. The employment of numerous participles causes the sense of a passage to be suspended until the end where the verb which forms the conclusion determines it.

Among the four systems that we have just sketched there are two which are diametrically opposed and which furnish the extreme points between which languages may oscillate. It is, on the one hand, the order parallel to grammatical *de*composition and that which places the qualifying word after the word qualified (le complément aprés le terme complété); on the other, the order which places first the governed word, then the governing word, and which is the exact counterpart of the analytical order. The first of these systems is pretty generally followed in French; the second is invariably observed by the Turkish and the Tartar languages. The German belongs about midway between the

two systems. The construction of the principal propositions
resembles that of the French in that the verb cuts the sentence
into two distinct parts, the subject and the attribute; the construction of subordinate sentences in which the verb is put at the
end and groups of words which end, with a few trifling exceptions, with the governing word brings it nearer the Turkish. The
English by virtue of its origin, partaking as it does of both the
German and Romance nature, naturally occupies a place interme-
diate between the German and the French. Finally, a language
which is totally different, the Chinese, may be put with the English in this abstract classification when one takes account only of
the constituent parts of the sentence.

The place of the verb.

All these variations may be summed up under two points of
view. We may consider, firstly, the place of the verb which
decides the physiognomy of the entire proposition; and, sec-
ondly, the arrangement of groups of words which determines the
form of the parts of the proposition. In respect to the verb it
may be said that our European languages are fond of placing it
between the subject and the attribute; the Tartar languages are
compelled to put it at the end of the proposition. The Latin also
has a manifest preference for the latter order.⁵ What is the difference between these constructions, if it be possible to discover
any? It will of course be understood that we are not here concerned about a fundamental difference in sense, but a characteristic shade which they imprint upon the sentence as a whole.
If there is any language which employs the two constructions and
which does not employ them indirectly but in cases strictly determined it would doubtless be of this language that we should ask a
solution of this problem. Now we have seen that in German the
nature of the proposition decides the place of the verb: the principal sentence corresponds to the French system, the subordinate
sentence to the Latin or even the Turkish system. Yet even in
the principal sentence, if the verb is in a compound tense the auxiliary alone stands in the middle of the sentence. At first sight

nothing seems more abnormal and arbitrary. Yet it may be that this strange appearance conceals a reasonable sense. What is the difference between a principal and a subordinate sentence? The principal sentence expresses a thought; it affirms. The subordinate sentence contains only a part of the idea expressed in the principal; it does not affirm. "Was the guilty love by which he is devoured already known in Athens?" (Ce coupable amour, dont il est dévorée, dans Athènes déjà s'était-il declaré?) Theseus believes that Hippolytus is devoured by a guilty love, but it is not that which he wishes to say, to affirm now. This is a known fact which enters as a partial idea into the question which he proposes and which is the object of the discourse. The principal sentence establishes a relation between two ideas, the subordinate sentence supposes this relation already established, it effaces the dichotomy of the thought. It is in this way if I mistake not that the difference between these two German constructions is to be explained.[6] The verb placed in the middle of the sentence in order to separate it and to bind together at the same time its two principal parts gives the proposition the form of a judgment which our modern languages show a tendency to claim for it. The sign of affirmation serves as a copula. Now, every time the verb is separated into constituent parts it is not the attributive but the abstract part which contains the affirmation. For this reason the auxiliary alone performs the functions and occupies the place of the copula. In subordinate sentences the copula gives up its characteristic position in order to indicate that these sentences do not embody a judgment which we utter in the instant of their enunciation, but, at most a judgment expressed at some previous time.

We believe then that wherever the verb occupies the middle place it is for the purpose of indicating that the whole thought contained in the entire proposition has been separated into two ideas, expressed by two groups of words, confusion between which is prevented by the interposed verb, and which are declared equal by an act of our judgment. Languages which put back the verb to the end of the sentence do not bring out so prominently the dichotomy and affirmative character of the proposition; the

Romance languages impress this character upon all kinds of propositions; the German obliterates it in subordinate propositions.

A usage established in many languages of fixed construction supports these observations. In French, in German, in English, and in nearly all the languages of Europe the subject is placed after the verb in interrogative sentences.[7] From our point of view this may be explained with entire satisfaction. In reality the interrogative proposition is not the total expression of a judgment; it is defective, and the judgment that it indicates is only completed by the answer. This is the reason why the affirmation in these propositions is not placed between the ideas of the subject and the attribute the union of which forms the total thought, but it is placed at the beginning to indicate that the sentence contains only the half of a judgment. The verb placed in the middle means, if I may be allowed so to express myself, that the two sides of the balance are in equilibrium; the verb placed at the beginning means that there is a weight lacking from one of the two sides and that the thought is not yet in equipoise.

Descending and ascending constructions.

Let us pass to the second point which divides languages with a fixed construction, that is, the arrangement of word-groups. We have seen that several languages give the governing word the precedence over the governed word; that certain others place the former after the latter; and that others again according to the nature of the complement follow one or the other of these usages. Which of these forms of procedure is the most reasonable? Our preferences incline rather toward the first which is represented by the Romance languages. To put the term *consequent* after the term *antecedent* seems to be logical: the opposite order has often been attacked as contrary to good sense. Yet the Turkish languages, the construction of which follows with rigorous exactness the second order of procedure, have their apologists and even admirers. M. A. L. Davids, in the introduction to his Turkish Grammar says " that the peculiar construction of the Turkish gives to its periods a weightiness and picturesque effect which add much to the dignity and expressiveness of the language"; and M. Davids but repeats in this matter the judgment of Sir W. Jones.[8] However much truth there may be in these eulogies we shall at least do well to be on our guard against condemnations of the genius of a language. That it may be lacking in logical precision in certain exceptional cases is to be admitted, but we should not readily believe that it sins against logic in a fundamental and well established rule. We shall not therefore pronounce against any of these systems, but try to discover what is the difference in character and what the effect it produces in discourse. This is what will guide us in our examination. General rules in most of these languages admit of certain exceptions the reasons for which we propose to study. The ancient languages are not rigidly held to any particular system, but this very liberty offers excellent facilities for comparison because it sanctions the employment of all these processes in turn. The first languages to be consulted are those which, while distinguishing different kinds of complements, have assigned special functions to each of the two opposite systems. We have already observed that there is in this regard a striking analogy between the Chinese and the English. The Chinese — for it may be well to repeat these details — appears to class its complements under three heads, viz., the complements of the substantive, the object of the verb, and the complements of circumstance of the verb (circumstantial complements of the verb).[9] The complements of the substantive are, in Chinese, held firmly to the order which we, to avoid circumlocutions, will name the order of ascending constructions. The objects of the verb are held to the order of descending constructions. The circumstantial complements more free in their construction, prefer nevertheless the first of these orders. English usage as we have stated above does not depart widely from these rules. The French even, although the descending construction might be considered a fundamental law of the language, approaches the Chinese by certain modifications which it admits into its system. The French places many adjectives before the substantive which they limit or define; it allows adverbs and adverbial expressions to precede the verb, but it is uncompromising in regard to the objective case. We are then authorized to distinguish two kinds of relations between the complementary or qualifying idea and the complemented or qualified idea. "To slay a man, to pay one's debt to his country." Here we have the relation of the action to the object upon which it is directed, a relation which is, so to speak, both sensible and material. "A large apartment." "To speak well" (*Bien parler*). Here we have a relation of grammatical definition which is not borrowed from the sensible world, but a more abstract relation that consists in restricting the comprehensiveness of an idea by attaching another idea to it.[10] In the former of these relations the two terms are more easily detached from each other and the imagination can picture to itself a progressive movement from the antecedent term to the consequent term. In the second there is only a decomposition of the idea effected by reflection in which the imagination no longer sees two different parts to which it may assign a priority and a posteriority. It is thus that we are able to explain why in many languages complements of the first class have a tendency to follow the idea to which they relate, and those of the second class to precede it. Adverbs and adverbial phrases are evidently placed between these two classes. Sometimes they belong to the first class, *bien parler;* sometimes to the second, *parler à peine* (To speak with difficulty). The principles that we have defined above are decisive for the Chinese construction, they prevail largely in the English, and to a considerable extent in French. We must therefore seek to establish a more general difference between the usages of construction.

Let us examine when it is necessary in French to depart from the general rule and to place the qualifying word before the word qualified. Articles and demonstrative pronouns — the man, this man, *l'homme, cet homme* — precede the substantive, pronouns in the objective case precede the verb. Descriptive epithets which do not serve to distinguish one individual from another but which bring out more conspicuously the most salient quality of the object under consideration, poetic epithets and such as are addressed chiefly to the imagination are usually placed before the substantive, as, "the brilliant light, the dark mud, dark cares." "No more money is needed to build an ugly prison than to make a house pleasant" (Voltaire).

It is evident that articles and determinative adjectives add an idea to the substantive which is closely connected with it in thought, and which one can detach from it only by an effort of abstraction. Further, the pronunciation so blends these complements with their substantives as to form almost one word with them. The union is a little less close between verbs and pronouns in the objective, but it is plainly to be seen; as soon as it is relaxed and the pronoun becomes in some degree independent, the order changes also, the pronoun assumes a full form and is placed after the verb. A like observation may also be made for qualifying adjectives. Those which only repeat in a more energetic and more animated manner the idea expressed by the substantive would naturally be expected to attach themselves much more closely than those which add a new idea."[11] "Judge then finally, readers wise, which is of most value, to worship God with simplicity, or" etc. If all readers were wise Voltaire would have said, "wise readers." It will be observed that the latter mode of expression forms a unity more nearly perfect than the former. There is a large number of expressions in which usage requires the adjective to precede the substantive because of the intimate connection, the complete fusion of the two ideas, 'a young man,' *juvenis*, *une fausse clef*, Greek αντίκλειθρον, German *Nachschlüssel*, where we express the compound idea with a single word.[12]

It is evident from these facts that the ascending construction binds more closely the ideas that have been put into relation with one another and that the descending construction tends more to detach them from one another. If we listen with attention it will be noticed that the voice passes more quickly from the adjective to the substantive and from the adverb to the verb in the phrases: *au second livre* (at the second book), *un glorieux souvenir* (a glorious memorial), *il a fortement appuyé sur ce passage* (he strongly emphasized this passage); that it passes from the substantive to the adjective and from the verb to the adverb when we say, *au livre second*, *un souvenir glorieux*, *il a appuyé fortement*. If there could be any doubt as to the truth of this remark one would only have to compare the familiar pronunciation of "froid extrême" in which the *d* is silent with the pronunciation of " profond abime" in which the *d* is heard. "Un savant aveugle" (a savant blind) (subst. adj.) is not pronounced like "un savant aveugle" (a learned blind man) (adj. subst.).[13]

In the arrangement of groups of words the German follows an order the opposite of the French; but exceptional terms of expression denote, by the peculiar character which is impressed upon them, the same principle and the same feeling. In German the ascending construction prevails, but if it sometimes uses the descending it is because the complement gains a greater independence by detaching itself more from the idea of the word which governs it. In French, we have seen, a contrary principle brings about a contrary exception: here we find an external sign of the difference in the pronunciation of the final consonant, whereas in German this sign is found in the inflection. The adjective placed before its substantive agrees with it in gender, number, and case, but its form undergoes no change when placed after the substantive. *Durch grosse, herrliche Thaten* (Through great, glorious deeds), but (through deeds great and glorious), *durch Thaten gross und herrlich*.

In effect, there is nothing more natural and nothing which can be more easily explained than this union more or less close between the two orders or kinds of construction. If you utter a word which depends on a word to come you are not allowed to make a pause; the attention is aroused, the mind is in suspense and demands that we give it the governing term, that on which the governed term may rest. If you utter first the word which governs others there is sometimes demanded a complement, but it is not demanded with such impatience; one can more easily content himself with what has been said whilst waiting to be fully satisfied. When saying for example *Scipio Carthaginem*, there is no point of repose. Here is an accusative floating in the air, so to speak. There is felt the need of resting somewhere, so give us forthwith a verb to support it — add *expugnavit*. If you begin the sentence with *Scipio expugnavit*, the mind wants to know the name of the city conquered by Scipio, yet from the grammatical point of view the words pronounced support each other and do not require any additional support. This fact is still more striking when the complements are not indispensable.

Examples taken from the ancient languages in which great freedom of construction is employed will shed still more light on the difference which we have pointed out. Lysias in his oration *De Pecuniis Publicis* begins his narrative with these words Ἐράτων, ὁ Ἐρασιφῶντος πατὴρ, ἐδανείσατο παρὰ τοῦ ἐμοῦ πάππου τάλαντα δύο. Here we have in succession the subject, the appositive, the verb, the complements of the verb. This is the analytical order just as we have it in French; it is even carried to an extent which cannot be imitated in French, for a numeral is put after a substantive to which it belongs and in place of saying 'two talents' the orator says "talents two." And directly afterwards he says Ἐπειδὴ δὲ ἐτελεύτησε καταλιπὼν υἱοὺς τρεῖς, Ἐρασιφῶντα καὶ Ἐράτωνα καὶ Ἐρασίστρατον. There is no doubt in regard to the character of these sentences. The orator is explaining a complicated pecuniary transaction and he endeavors to do it in such a way that his auditors, the judges, may be able to follow him easily from point to point. For this reason he does not interlink the elements of the sentence as the ancient authors are in the habit of doing, but relaxes the bonds that unite them in order to follow the descending construction. As a result of this arrangement there occur rests between the words, and the delivery of the sentence may be compared to a liquid which is not poured out at once, but which is caused to flow out drop by drop. Now change the order of the words and put Ἐράτων παρὰ τοῦ ἐμοῦ πάππου δύο τάλαντα ἐδανείσατο, or Δύο παρὰ τοῦ ἐμοῦ πάππου Ἐράτων τάλαντα ἐδανείσατο — its characteristic analytical exposition has disappeared. The beginning of the Republic of Plato is cited by the ancients[14] themselves as an example of the decomposed order, and it is precisely that of the descending construction. Κατέβην χθὲς εἰς τὸν Πειραιᾶ μετὰ Γλαύκωνος τοῦ Ἀρίστωνος προσευξόμενός τε τῇ θεῷ (I went down yesterday into the Peiraeus with etc.).[15]

Let us cite Lysias again (contra Phil. § 18): Ὁρμώμενος γὰρ ἐξ Ὠροποῦ, περιὼν κατὰ τοὺς ἀγροὺς, καὶ ἐντυγχάνων τῶν πολιτῶν τοῖς πρεσβυτάτοις ... τούτους ἀφῃρεῖτο τὰ ὑπάρχοντα. (Setting out from Oropus and going about the country he sought out the most aged citizens and deprived them of their property.) This last example is descriptive; the participles precede in order to add to the vivacity of the picture which the speaker is slowly unfolding before our eyes.

Numeral adjectives especially are very often placed after their substantives when it is important to be exact. Examples are abundant in Xenophon and Cæsar: (Ἐντεῦθεν ἐξελαύνει σταθμοὺς δύο, παρασάγγας δέκα. Ἐνταῦθα ἔμεινεν ἡμέρας τρεῖς, etc.). The aborigines of Aristophanes in the Symposium of Plato have χεῖρας τέτταρας, πρόσωπα δύο, κεφαλὴν μίαν, ὦτα τέτταρα, αἰδοῖα δύο. Our languages cannot attain this precision of expression. The ascending order shows us a contrary character. Ὡς μὲν οὖν δεῖ τὰ προσήκοντα ποιεῖν ἐθέλοντας ὑπάρχειν ἅπαντας ἑτοίμως, ὡς ἐγνωκότων ὑμῶν καὶ πεπεισμένων, παύομαι λέγων (Dem. Phil. I. 43). (The first clause is the object of λέγων, and ἐθέλοντας ὑπάρχειν as often in Dem. is hardly different in meaning from ἐθέλειν.) One does not follow tranquilly these closely connected sentences, but is carried by main force to the finale.

But the most striking examples of the descending construction are found in the definitions of Aristotle, that great analytic genius who invented a purely philosophical language for the Greeks, and who, by his new forms of expression as much perhaps as by his method and his universal knowledge, appears to have prepared the way for modern science. If among all the remains of antiquity there is nothing that so nearly approaches the French construction as the definitions of Aristotle, would not this fact indicate that those who speak thus have reflecting and methodical minds? Here are some examples drawn from his Rhetoric: Ἀρετή ἐστι δύναμις ποριστικὴ ἀγαθῶν καὶ φυλακτική, καὶ δύναμις εὐεργατικὴ πολλῶν καὶ μεγάλων, καὶ πάντων περὶ πάντα. (Virtue is the faculty which provides us with what is good and preserves it to us; it is also a faculty capable of benefiting us in many and important matters, even every object in every respect.)

Ἔστι δ' ἔπαινος λόγος ἐμφανίζων μέγεθος ἀρετῆς. (Eulogy is a discourse which sets forth the grandeur of virtue.) Ἀνάγκη φίλον εἶναι τὸν συνηδόμενον τοῖς ἀγαθοῖς καὶ συναλγοῦντα τοῖς λυπηροῖς, μὴ διά τι ἕτερον ἀλλὰ δι' ἐκεῖνō. (Of necessity to be a friend to any one is to rejoice with him in his good fortune and grieve with him in his sorrows, not from some other cause but for his sake.)

The philosopher decomposes the idea which he wishes to define, and while putting before you the result of this intellectual toil he likewise passes in review one by one the elements of this idea in their most developed state and as little as possible interlocked with one another. This is his manner of procedure when he frames a definition. But when at a subsequent time he comes back again to this definition he does not follow the order of the first analysis. The elements which make up the idea being already known, and the mind of the reader having been familiarized with them, the author feels free to give a greater degree of unity to his expression and to present under a more compact form the parts which at first needed to be shown separate and distinct from each other. When he gives for the first time the oft repeated definition of tragedy he expresses himself in these terms:

Ἔστιν οὖν τραγῳδία μίμησις πράξεως σπουδαίας καὶ τελείας (Tragedy then is an imitation of an action important and complete) (Poetic, chap. 6), — the words of the original preserving exactly the same order with the French [and the English]. But when he subsequently refers to this definition he renders it as follows: Κεῖται δ' ἡμῖν τὴν τραγῳδίαν τελείας καὶ ὅλης πράξεως εἶναι μίμησιν. The Greek uses the liberty which the laws of his language allow him, and without changing the terms, solely by the manner in which he arranges them, he collects into a bundle what he had at first exhibited by piecemeal: he puts before us as a totality what he had at first decomposed into its constituent parts. This shade in the difference of meaning cannot be represented in French. The same thing is seen in chap. 11, where the definition of the peripetia is given: Ἐστὶν δὲ περιπέτεια ἡ εἰς τὸ ἐναντίον τῶν πραττομένων μεταβολή, καθάπερ εἴρηται.[16] (The peripetia, as has already been defined, is an unexpected reverse of fortune in the persons acting, necessarily or probably arising from the incident.)

One rarely finds in Plato definitions so well developed and bearing the stamp of careful analysis. Plato is not fond of minute analysis. He seeks to bind together, to construct; he strives after unity. Accordingly when there are terms in his works which come near to being definitions, he expresses himself in language which is almost the exact opposite of that which we have seen in Aristotle: his words when taken together form a well-rounded whole. This is his definition of poetry or rather of ποίησις: Ἡ ἐκ τοῦ μὴ ὄντος εἰς τὸ ὂν ἰόντι ὁτωοῦν αἰτία πᾶσά ἐστι ποίησις. (All creation or passage of non-being into being is poetry or making.)

We read in the Phaedo this definition of death, Ἡ τῆς ψυχῆς ἀπὸ τοῦ σώματος ἀπαλλαγή, which Cicero translates after the manner of Aristotle, *Discessus animi a corpore*. Rhetoric is, according to Plato, πολιτικῆς μορίου εἴδωλον (Gorgias, p. 463 D.), which is exactly rendered by Quintilian, II, 15, 25, with the words *Civilitatis particulae simulacrum* (A semblance of a division of the political art). It is impossible to imitate in French [or indeed in any analytical language] the rapidity of the Greek. We must say, "la rhétorique est la simulacre d'une partie de la politique." Pronounce "le simulacre d'une partie de la politique" as rapidly as you may wish, yet there will be pauses of voice between the words which are neither in the Greek nor the Latin. The reason of this difference is found in the succession of words. The ladder of grammatical dependence is peculiar in this that one ascends it rapidly and descends it at his leisure.

What is the most perfect construction?

Briefly expressed, the chief characteristic of the ascending construction is to make prominent the unity of the thought, that of the descending construction is to show clearly all its parts. Both systems have their conspicuous advantages, but they have also their drawbacks. If carried to extremes the first would become obscure, involved, and would require an effort to follow the details of the thought; the second would break up the unity of the thought and consequently destroy the energy and beauty of expression.

The French language has adopted the system of descending construction, but it has preserved a prudent mean in the application of the system. It is for this reason that it has become the language of conversation *par excellence*, for it is in conversation that it is specially important to make one's self understood with the greatest rapidity and ease."[17] But without modifications and restrictions upon this system, the thought would escape in the very process of development. Suppose we have phrases of considerable length in which all the words should be ranked in their appropriate order in the syntactic hierarchy; they will be found to be diffuse and languishing. Translate, for example, while scrupulously observing this principle, the following phrase of moderate length: Ἐπιθυμήσαντος τοῦ δήμου παρὰ τοὺς νόμους ἐννέα στρατηγοὺς μιᾷ ψήφῳ ἀποκτεῖναι πάντας (Xen. Mem. I, 1), "Le peuple désirant mettre à mort tous les neuf généraux par un seul vote malgré les lois." (The people desiring to put to death all the nine generals by a single vote contrary to the laws.) The unity disappears, the sentence is dissolved. It is necessary to forcibly break loose from the system and to put first some of the complements of the verb. "Le peuple voulant, malgré les lois, mettre à mort par un seul vote les neuf généraux à la fois." And still the sentence is somewhat languishing. Let us compare the two passages which follow — one from Rousseau, the other from Voltaire: "Que chacun d'eux découvre à son tour son cœur au pied de ton trône avec la même sincerité." (Let each one of them reveal in his turn his heart at the foot of thy throne with the same sincerity.) "Ceux qui vont en guenilles, d'un bout du royaume à l'autre, arracher des passants, par des cris lamentables, de quoi aller au cabaret." (Those who go in tatters from one end of the kingdom to the other to extort from the passers-by, through their pitiable cries, the wherewithal to go to the pot-house.) To me the sentence of Voltaire seems finer, rounder and more finished. It is not however shorter, not less complex than that of Rousseau. But in the former the principle of the order of the objectives is too scrupulously observed, which produces a construction without unity. In the latter the auxiliary *to go* has been used for the purpose of placing some complements before the verb. It seems to me the sentence would gain in point of construction if it were changed in an analogous manner, for example: "Que chacun vienne à son tour au pied de ton trône découvrir son cœur avec la même sincerité." Often the remedy is still more simple, for usage allows us to begin a sentence with a circumstantial complement and to place it in a measure outside of the syntactic framework. Generally speaking, complicated sentences, in which there are many members dependent upon one another are not good if arranged exclusively according to the descending construction. The French accordingly rejects them, or rather while allowing them, it refuses to descend quietly the rounds of grammatical dependence and binds the sentence by methods like those of the ancient and the Germanic languages.

The German, on the other hand, the construction of which is essentially ascending, often rejects this principle from an opposite motive. It does this in order to relax the bonds of the sentence, to bring out prominently a particular point. In such cases the German allows the inversion of descending construction. *Wer wird hier leben wollen ohne Freiheit?* in place of *Wer wird hier ohne Freiheit leben wollen?* (Who will be willing to live here without liberty?) A complement is placed after the governing term which according to the rule ought to terminate the sentence.

It appears then that the perfection of a language consists not in following invariably an exclusive system of construction, or in adhering with immutable logic to the ultimate consequences of an adopted principle; but, on the contrary, it consists in a judicious improvement upon a too prominent and uniform characteristic, by the admission of an opposite system and by balancing the shortcomings of one method over against the excellences of another. It is by so doing that the French and German have avoided extremes. The Turkish adheres tenaciously to the ascending construction, even to the extent of placing prepositions after nouns. It applies the same system to groups of words, to propositions and to periods, and may therefore be regarded as the most consistent of languages in point of construction. But has this consistency been an advantage to the Turkish language? has it made it better adapted to the faithful interpretation of thought? This is of course a matter for competent judges to decide, but we may well doubt it. And this, not because the system of ascending construction is in itself to be condemned, for it is neither more nor less so than the contrary system, but to put speech in bondage to an exclusive system, be it what it may, I regard as a defect and an imperfection in a language. If we adopt this view of the case, we are necessarily led to place in the front rank those languages which place the fewest shackles on construction, and to regard the Greek and the Latin as the most perfect languages in this respect because they are the most free.

Constructions in the free languages.

Now that we have again returned to the classic languages, let us try, as it is necessary to the completeness of this study, to bring even their irregularities or liberties under some sort of a classification. Every time that several words concur to express an idea we can distinguish, by examining carefully the syntax, four or even five different ways in which words can be arranged in the classic languages. The complement follows the word or term on which it depends (*avidus gloriae*); this is what we have named the *descending construction*. The complement precedes the word on which it depends (*vini plenum*); this is the *ascending construction*. When the complement is followed by the word qualified and preceded by a word which is indissolubly bound to it we shall call it the order of *enclavement* or inlocked construction. When the complement is separated from the word next to which the rules of syntax require it to be placed, by another word or by several words which constitute part of another syntactic group, we have what we may call the dispersed construction: let us however retain for it the name which it has always borne, namely, *hyperbaton*. We may add as a fifth form the cases where the words which are used to express an idea are joined into a single word. It is true that a compound is not properly speaking a fact of syntax; and yet it is not wholly foreign to our subject, because the same ideas which in one language are expressed by compound words are sometimes rendered in another by groups of words.[18] Arranging then these five constructions according to the connection more or less close, of partial ideas which are their elements, we shall have in the first place the compound word which indicates the closest union; second, the *enclavement* or inlocking; third, the ascending construction; fourth, the descending construction; fifth, the hyperbaton, which places the widest space between ideas as between words. The Greek on account of its admirable flexibility can employ the same terms in all the five forms. As it is very difficult to find an entirely suitable example in their writers we shall take the risk of proposing one of our own. The poet-musician who instructed a Greek chorus for their imposing festivals was called χοροδιδάσκαλος. The idea is expressed in the most perfect unity by a compound and continuous word. If we wished to distinguish the two ideas which are fused in the compound word, preserving at the same time the unity of the conception, we should use the form of the enclave. "It is not necessary that we should put in the same rank him who bears the expense of the representation and him who teaches the chorus." In Greek we should express this about as follows: Τόν εἰς τὴν χορηγίαν δαπανῶντα οὐκ εἰς τὴν αὐτὴν τάξιν δεῖ τιθέναι τῷ τοῦ χοροῦ διδασκάλῳ. The complement τοῦ χοροῦ is inclosed between the substantive διδασκάλῳ and its article. The ideas connected with choragus and chorodidascalus are somewhat developed to make prominent the import of the two functions, nevertheless the elements of these ideas are bound into a fascicle. The following is an example of the third form. "We can predict the success of a chorus, if we know the musical talent of him who instructs it." Προλέγοις ἄν πῶς ἀγωνιεῖται ὁ χορός, εἰ τοῦ χοροῦ τὸν διδάσκαλον γνοίης μουσικῆς ὅπως ἔχει.

If we wished to make very prominent one of two ideas and to pass lightly over the other we should only have to separate more the elements of the group by making use of the fifth construction, namely the hyperbaton: εἰ τὸν διδάσκαλον γνοίης τοῦ χοροῦ ὅπως ἔχει περὶ μουσικῆς. Finally, to give an example of the descending or analytical construction, one might reply to the question: What is the chorodidascalus? by Ἀλλὰ φανερὸν ὅτι εἴη ἄν ὁ διδάσκαλος τοῦ χοροῦ, ὡς αὐτὸ τὸ ὄνομα δηλοῖ.

What distinguishes these five forms of expression from each other, I make haste to add, is not simply the more or less close connection between ideas placed in relation to each other; there are slight shades of another kind to which we will return in the third chapter. But we have not yet exhausted all the constructions so remarkably varied which are at the disposal of the Greek language. The ingenious use which this language makes of the article gives it a sixth form, that of the explanatory appositive, which, considered in relation to the connection of ideas, can be placed between numbers two and three. In this form the article is repeated as ὁ διδάσκαλος ὁ τοῦ χοροῦ.

Let us add some observations on each of these constructions, omitting however the ascending and descending, of which we have already spoken. Regarding compound words it may be said that they exhibit a twofold union of elements: one in which the determinative part precedes the part that is determined or limited, (ζωγράφος, *ignivomus*, beau-frère, Blumenkrone) and the other in which these relations are reversed (ῥίψασπις, crève-cœur, Taugenichts). We have here again the difference between the ascending and descending constructions. But if the former of these constructions binds the elements much more closely than the second, and if the compound word is the closest possible union between two ideas, we may wonder how there can be words which follow the second of these processes. In reality a very large majority of Greek compounds belongs to the former class. In German there are not many of the second class and these were evidently so far as we can judge at first short phrases like the French va-nu-pieds. In Latin they scarcely exist (*verticordia*, perhaps *versipellis*),[19] at least there is no reason to reckon among compound words *res publica*, *jus jurandum* and similar expressions. The French language, on the contrary, in nearly all its compounds places the determining word after the determined or limited word. But this anomaly which grows out of the analytical character of the language is in perfect accordance with general considerations. French compounds form in reality a unity which is much less complete than Greek, German, or Latin compounds: they are not strictly speaking real compounds. Even their orthography is evidence of this since it requires their elements to be separated by a hyphen.

The enclosed or inlocked construction is much used in the ancient languages, particularly the Greek. When the language affords neither a simple nor a compound word for the expression of an idea it becomes necessary to decompose this idea and express it by several words. In order to obliterate as far as possible this *de*composition, to bring together as closely as possible the two elements the ancients used the enclosed[20] construction. There are in Greek no terms corresponding to the Latin *patruus* and *avunculus:* θεῖος means uncle, in general. In order to designate specifically the maternal uncle Xenophon says (Cyrop. I, 3, 12), τὸν πάππον ἢ τὸν τῆς μητρὸς ἀδελφόν. He says also, to designate a prince, the son of a king (II, 1, 13) ὑπὸ βασιλέως τε παιδὸς καὶ ὑπὸ στρατηγοῦ. In the two phrases simple terms are co-ordinated with complex ones: this was one reason more for giving to these last the most compact form. The same thing may be seen in Latin. We read in the oration *pro lege Manilia* (chap. 3), *Uno nuntio atque una litterarum significatione;* and (chap. 9), *In ipso illo malo gravissimaque belli offensione.* The enclave has preserved the symmetry of the expression. The use of the article puts the advantage still more on the side of the Greek. Compare, for example, these two sentences of Plato (Soph. 254, A), τὰ τῆς τῶν πολλῶν ψυχῆς ὄμματα καρτερεῖν πρὸς τὸ θεῖον ἀφορῶντα ἀδύνατα (The eyes of most men can not endure sight of divinity), and (Symp. p. 182, D), διὰ τὴν τῶν θεμένων τῆς ψυχῆς ἀργίαν (Owing to the sluggishness of soul of those proposing the law). There are in these two examples three partial ideas which concur in the formation of one single idea, but the relations of these two ideas are different in the two cases. This gives us the reason why the articles are differently placed. In the first example the intermediary idea of ψυχή is joined equally to the idea which it governs and to that upon which it depends; in the second it is joined to that upon which it depends. The first may be translated, the organ of ordinary intelligence; the second, the intellectual inertness of legislators.

Such is then the force of the enclave that it can take the place of inflection. It is well known that in Greek, adverbs and adverbial phrases placed between the substantive and its article may be construed as adverbs, οἱ νῦν ἄνθρωποι. Πρὸς τοῦ κακίστου κἀκ κακῶν Ὀδυσσέως (Soph. Phil. 384) (By the basest of the base, Ulysses). *Heri semper lenitas* is a hellenism hazarded by Terence. But we can very well say, *Caesaris in Hispania res secundae,* in Latin.

We can very properly limit ourselves here to a single group in regard to the construction which disperses the component parts of a syntactic group. *Animorum nulla in terris origo inveniri potest* (Cic. Tusc. I, 27) (For the souls of men no origin can be found in the earth). It is evident that the two ideas *animorum* and *origo*, though connected by their syntax, are separated in thought as they are in the order of words. *Animorum* is the point of departure while *origo* forms part of what we have called the goal of the sentence. On the other hand the adverbial expression *in terris*, which is enclosed within *nulla* and *origo* is joined to these words and almost forms with them one and the same idea, even if it have not the grammatical form of an adjective. It is almost as if one should say in French, Pour les âmes, ou ne peut en découvrir aucune origine terrestre. We shall return to this construction in the third chapter.

The period.

Thus far we have only considered the simple proposition. When the framework of the thought is enlarged, when its parts are represented by partial propositions, the whole will form a compound proposition or period. The period which differs from the simple proposition in the extent and development of its constituent elements does not differ from it in its essence: in it are found the same shades of construction that we have just pointed out. Nevertheless the process which is followed in our modern languages for the arrangement of simple propositions is not entirely adhered to for that of the period. In this respect there is a freedom akin to that allowed in the ancient languages. So true is this in French that if we wish to escape the tyranny of the analytic order we detach a word from the proposition and give to this word the form of a member of the sentence. "C'est à vous que je veux parler" (It is to you that I wish to speak). "Ce désastre, je l'ai prédit depuis longtemps" (As to this disaster, I have predicted it for a long time). A form analogous to this last allows us to put the incident which occupies the place of the direct object at the beginning of the sentence. "Que vous soyez mon ami, je veux le croire; mais je ne puis admettre que" . . . (That you are my friend, I am willing to believe; but I cannot admit that . . .). When one part of an entire thought is raised to the rank of a subordinate proposition our languages release it, so to speak, from the rules of construction and do not rigorously fix its place. We may well congratulate ourselves on this freedom without which the oratorical art would not have attained that perfection which is both our pleasure and our admiration.

Nothing is easier than to exhibit the ascending, the descending, and the inlocked construction, as also the hyperbaton, in the disposal of the parts of the period. One needs only to open the funeral discourses of Bossuet to find abundant examples; and the various characteristics aimed at in these constructions can even be distinguished. We give some periods the principal parts of which are arranged in the descending order of syntax. "Mon esprit, rebuté de tant d'indignes traitements qu'on a faits à la majesté et à la vertu, ne se résoudrait jamais à se jeter parmi tants d'horreurs si la constance admirable avec laquelle cette princesse a soutenu ses calamités ne surpassait de bien loin les crimes qui les ont causées." (My spirit, repelled by so many indignities done to majesty and virtue, would never have had the courage to cast itself among so many horrors, if the wonderful constancy with which this princess bore her misfortunes did not surpass by far the crimes which caused them.) "C'était un dégoût secret de tout ce qui a de l'autorité et une démangeaison d'innover sans fin après qu'on en a vu le premier exemple." (It was a secret distaste for everything connected with authority and an inordinate desire for innovation without end after they saw the first example of it.) In the following period we perceive a much more closely connected whole, a more finished unity, more perfection in fine; and the construction is ascending. "Soit qu'il élève les trônes, soit qu'il les abaisse, soit qu'il communique sa puissance aux princes, soit qu'il la retire à lui-même et ne leur laisse que leur propre faiblesse, il leur apprend leur devoir d'une manière souveraine et digne de lui." (Whether he exalted thrones, whether he humbled them, whether he imparted his power to princes, whether he withdrew it to himself and left them to their own weakness, he taught them their duty in the manner of a sovereign and one that was worthy of him.)[21]

The ancient rhetoricians had carefully noted this difference. Hermogenes designates with the name πλαγιασμός that which we have called the ascending construction. One experiences, says he, a kind of uneasiness from the commencement of periods of this kind (ταραχὴ γάρ τις εὐθὺς ἐγγίνεται); the frame of the thought being very large, the expression will not be really clear because the sense is so long suspended.[22] The following is an example of πλαγιασμός taken from an ancient orator (Cic. pro lege Manil. 22): *Deinde etiamsi qui sunt pudore ac temperantia moderatiores tamen eos esse tales propter multitudinem cupidorum hominum nemo arbitratur.* (Then, albeit there are those who are more held in restraint by shame and self-control yet no one thinks they are such, etc.)

This is the ascending construction. The following is a freer kind of descending construction (Ibid. 3): *Verumtamen illis imperatoribus laus est tribuenda, quod egerunt; venia danda, quod reliquerunt propterea quod ab eo bello Sullam in Italiam res publica, Murenam Sulla revocavit.* (But indeed to those generals praise is to be given for what they did, pardon is to be granted for what they left undone, because, etc.)

Let us return to French eloquence and let us borrow from it an example of the enclosed (enclavée) construction. "Elle vit avec étonnement que Dieu qui avait rendu inutiles tant d'entreprises et tant d'efforts, parce qu'il attendait l'heure qu'il avait marquée, quand elle fut arrivée alla prendre comme par la main le roi, son fils, pour le conduire à son trône." (She saw with astonishment that God, who had made vain so many undertakings and so many efforts, because he was waiting for the hour he had appointed, when it was come, went to take as by the hand the king her son to lead him to the throne.) It is this construction that Cicero introduces in the expression of a thought of Gracchus. The orator of the second century before our era had said: *Abesse non potest quin ejusdem hominis sit probos improbare, qui improbos probet;* that of the first corrects thus: *Abesse non potest quin ejusdem hominis sit, qui improbos probet, probos improbare.* He calls this correction, *in quadrum redigere, efficere aptum quod fuerat antea diffluens ac solutum* (Cic. Orat. 70).

Let us add, finally, a very happy use of the hyperbaton, if it be allowed to designate by this term the disarrangement, not of the words which enter into a syntactic group, but of the partial propositions that enter into a period. "Malgré les mauvais succès de

ses armes infortunées, si on a pu le vaincre, on n'a pu le forcer."
(Notwithstanding the ill success of his unlucky arms, if they were able to vanquish him, they could not compel him.)

Whatever individuality there is in the construction of Greek and Latin periods appertains largely to certain oratorical forms with which we need not occupy ourselves here. But the character of the two classic languages is in a great measure determined by the vast proportions the period may assume in them. Owing to their synthetic character each of the elements of the period, each piece that enters into this beautiful architecture, is more complex and more important than in our modern languages. Thus the sentences which contain an accusative as the subject of an infinitive become in our translations compound sentences; but it is a mistake to consider them such in Greek and Latin. They may be taken as amplified sentences, but they do not cease to be essentially simple. *Plurimum dicit oratori conferre Theophrastus lectionem poetarum* (Quint. X, I, 27). In translating this sentence either into English or French we are compelled to make the object of *dicit* a relative clause: — Th. says (that) the reading of the poets, etc. The arrangement of the words shows the sentence to be as simple as in, "I have seen two regiments depart." The ancients go one step farther. They often interweave the words of a relative clause with those of the principal proposition in such a way as to give unity to a sentence that is in reality compound. What is known as attraction, and is so often met with in Greek, mingles yet more completely the two propositions and fuses as it were the one with the other. *Quod quoniam, in quo sit, magna dissensio est* (Cic. de Fin. V, 6). (Regarding which, since there is great diversity of opinion in what it (the highest good) consists.)[23] Τοτὲ μὲν δὴ τοῦτον τὸν τρόπον εἶχε τὰ πράγματ' ἐκείνοις, χρωμένοις οἷς εἶπον προστάταις. Ἀλλ' ὅσης ἅπαντες ὁρᾶτ' ἐρημίας ἐπειλημμένοι . . . ἀπεστερήμεθα μὲν χώρας οἰκείας (Dem. Olynth. III, 27) (οἷς εἶπον whom I mentioned, for οὓς εἶπον). (This then is the state in which they found their affairs in those times when they used those I have named as leaders. But ye all see with what solitude we are encompassed . . . we are deprived of our own territory.)

The Romans before studying Greek models had already found

a period which was peculiarly their own, one that was wholly ascending, and which though comprehensive and stately, was heavy and involved. It is found in the most ancient decrees of the Senate and people of Rome, and we will cite here a few examples which may likewise serve to illustrate what we have said above in regard to the construction of the Tartar languages. In fact nothing can more nearly resemble the general cast of the Turkish period than these sentences taken from an agrarian law of the year 643 A.U.C. *Quei* (qui) *ager publicus populi. Romanei* (-i) *in terra Italia P. Mucio L. Calpurnio consulibus, fuit de eo agro loco quem agrum locum populus ex publico in privatum commutavit, quo pro agro loco ex privato in publicum tantum modum agri locei* (-i) *commutavit, is ager locus domneis* (-inis) *privatus ita, uti quoi* (cui) *optima lege privatus sit, esto. Qui ager locus in Africa est quei Romae publice venieit* (-iit) *venieritve, quod ejus agri loci, quei populeis libereis* (nom. plur.) *in Africa sunt, quei eorum in ameicitiam populi Romanei bello Paenicio proxsumo manserunt, queive..., quisque eorum habuerunt,... pro eo agro loco II vir ...facito... detur assignetur.* Each partial sentence is subordinated to the sentence which follows it and in a measure becomes part of it so that the general idea stated at the beginning is more and more restricted; in like manner each one of these little sentences ends with its verb, and the complete period is closed and sealed with the principal verb. These old constructions so thoroughly Latin are again found, shorter and less heavy, among the classic authors. Cicero writes, "*Si hoc statueris, quarum laudum gloriam adamaris, quibus artibus eae laudes comparantur, in iis esse elaborandum*" (Ad Fam. II, 4). Here *in iis* takes up *quibus artibus* just before, and *eae laudes* repeats in another form *quarum laudum* of the preceding line.

Nam philosophandi scientiam concedens multis, quod est oratoris propriam, apte, distincte, ornate dicere, quoniam in eo studio aetatem consumpsi, si id mihi assumo, videor id meo jure quodammodo vindicare (De Offic. I, 1, 4). (While I may have less skill than others in philosophizing I may with justice claim to be a firstrate orator, because I have devoted myself to that branch particularly.) Many similar examples may be readily found. In the following example from Cic. *de lege agraria* the relation of the conditional sentences to each other is exactly the same as that of the relative sentences cited above. *Neque si qui agros populo romano pollicentur, si (ea pollicentes) aliud quiddam obscure moliuntur, aliud spe ac specie simulationis ostentant, populares existimandi sunt* (De lege agr. II, 4). Here Cicero expresses himself just like the most ancient Latin monuments. The XII tables have *Si nox furtum factum sit, si im (qui id furtam fecerit) occisit jure caesus esto.* See Macrobius, Saturn, I, 4, 19.

---

[1] Professor Charles Short has discussed quite fully the Order of Words in Attic Prose in Yonge's English-Greek Lexicon, published by Harper & Bros. The inquiry is, however, of little interest because of the impossibility of formulating results. In Greek perhaps more than in any other language it is the thoughts which determine the order of words, and as the thoughts of scarcely two writers are the same their arrangement of words will also be different. Emphasis too varies greatly and the language imposes but little restraint on the order of words.

[2] The attributive part of the verb is sometimes a past participle, sometimes an infinitive. The past participle was originally an adjective, and our French poets still say archaistically, "La première épée dont s'est armé Rodrigue, a sa trame coupée" (*hat seinen lebensfaden durchschnitten*). We read in Joinville, chap. 87, "Pour ce que je ne veil que nulz face jamez bien pour le guerredon de paradis avoir, ne pour la poour d'enfer; mez proprement pour l'amour de Dieu avoir, qui tant vaut et qui tout le bien nous peut faire." [Here we find three clauses ending with three infins., viz., avoir, avoir and faire. In modern French this construction is no longer admissible. We should probably have, pour avoir la recompense de Paradis, and, peut nous faire tout le bien.] We may translate these lines into German without changing the place of a single word: they are all arranged according to the rules of German construction. Generally speaking the two languages seem to have had more points of similarity during the Middle Ages than they have at present. In German when a part of the attribute is placed at the beginning of the sentence the verb should precede the subject; the same rule holds good when this part of the attribute assumes the form of an initial phrase. The rule is less rigid in old French, but it is generally observed. "En ce point nous envoia le soudane son conseil pour parler à nous." (*In diesem Augenblick schickte uns der Sultan....*) Joinville, chap. 66, "Après ce que le viell home s'en fu allé, qui nous ot reconfortez, revint le conseil le soudane à nous." (*Nachdem ... kamen die Raethe....*) Modern French has preserved some traces of these constructions, which in truth are entirely natural and found in very many languages. "Ainsi parla le roi"

(Thus spoke the king). "Déjà prenait son essor . . . cet aigle. . . ." It is on the same principle that "il dit" becomes "dit-il" (*sagte er*, said he), and "le voisin repondit" becomes "repondit le voisin" (*antwortete der Nachbar*, replied the neighbor). This takes place when these brief phrases are preceded by some of the quoted words, in other words, by a part of their complement. W.

³ See Abel Remusat, *Elements de la grammaire chinoise*, Paris 1822, §§ 78, 79, 80, 95, 158, 159, 177. What we have said regarding the Chinese refers to the *ancient style*. W.

⁴ See A. Remusat, *Recherches sur les langues tartares*, Paris 1820, Vol. I, pp. 118 and 279. Davids, A Grammar of the Turkish Language. Londres 1832. The examples given are from these two works. W. An excellent brief manual is The Turkish Vade-Mecum of the Ottoman Colloquial Language. London 1882.

⁵ Quintilian IX, IV, 26. "*Verbo sensum cludere multo, si compositio patiatur, optimum est. In verbis enim sermonis vis.*" Dichotomy is a section or division into two parts.

⁶ In this matter I follow the hints given by Herling, *Syntaxe de la langue allemande* I, §§ 36, 44.

⁷ In French the noun-subject precedes the interrogative verb ("Le vice est-il un mal?"), but the pronoun indicates the place of the subject. The noun-subject in this case makes sense by itself almost like the first words of a sentence beginning with a pathetic passage like the following, "Le vice, detestez-le toujours." W.

⁸ Davids, p. XLVII. Sir W. Jones, Asiatic Researches, II, p. 360.

⁹ We ought perhaps to crave the indulgence of the reader for employing a terminology which does not properly apply to the Chinese. But we are speaking less of this language than of a system of construction which might as well be found in any other language. W.

¹⁰ See the Lettre à M. Abel Remusat, par M. G. de Humboldt, 1827, p. 41.

¹¹ We find in Greek epic poetry a usage that confirms this statement. If there exist any literary works in which picturesque adjectives abound it is unquestionably the poems of Homer and Hesiod. Men had become so accustomed to observe certain substantives always accompanied by the same adjectives or epithets that they finally used the epithet without the noun. Thus, ἡ γλαύκη designates the sea, ἡ φερέοικος the snail. The two ideas were so commingled as ultimately to be regarded as one. In this the poets simply renewed a procedure that is plainly evident in the beginnings of language. Things received their names from some quality or action peculiar to them and which for this reason impressed the human mind most forcibly (substantives are derived from verbs and from adjectives). The serpent has its name from its tortuous gait. But when subsequently that which was significant in a name became obscured and names themselves became more and more signs with a purely conventional value, having ceased to reflect an image of a human thought, the poets reanimated their language by adding to the conventional sign an expressive and living epithet sometimes even going so far as to substitute the epithet for the sign. W.

The origin of all names is to be sought in the same direction. It may be said further that the use of descriptive adjectives as nouns is by no means confined to the Greek. The English furnishes many examples though in most cases the original meaning is not patent. The theory held by philologists generally in regard to the origin of language is that its simplest elements are the significant roots spoken of above which roots are the expression of a general concept. For example, the root ἑρπ, *serp*, and *sarp* has the meaning 'creep or crawl' in Greek, Latin, and Sanskrit. Our word 'foot' has cognates in many Aryan languages. Its simplest form is the Zend and Sanskrit *pad* meaning 'go' or 'go to.' The same is true of the English word 'wit,' the cognates of which are even more numerous. Its primitive signification is 'see.'

[12] "Un brave homme" (a good kind man), "un galant homme" (an honest man), are old phrases that may be regarded as single words almost as much as "prud'homme" (expert) and "gentilhomme" (gentleman, in the British sense). If the adjective has a more definite and modern meaning we say "un homme brave" (a brave man), "un homme galant" (a ladykiller). For the same reason we say "de fines gens" and "des gens bien fins." When closely connected with the substantive that it precedes, the adjective retains the gender of the Latin *gentes* which is feminine, but placed after the noun it conforms to the modern usage. The original sense having been lost sight of it has come to be regarded as masculine. W. There are in all languages certain words that are regarded as simple but which in an earlier stage of the language were compounds. In English there are a good many words as to which we are in doubt whether to write them with or without a hyphen.

The peculiarity of this word the gender of which is determined by the position of the adjective that accompanies it may have arisen from the struggle between the gender of the Latin original and the natural gender of the idea which it expresses, namely, men, individuals. This struggle ended in a sort of compromise, or we might say it was a drawn battle. In the end usage established the rule as above given. In the other Romance languages the descendants of *gens* retained the original gender.

[13] Compare the English 'a blackbird' with 'a black bird,' gentle man or noble man, with gentleman and nobleman.

[14] Demetrius *de Elocutione*, Vol. IX, p. 13 of the edition of Walz.

[15] Cf. note [13] on p. 50.

[16] The two final words show that the author refers to a definition given in some former part of the work, but this is not found in any extant text.

[17] "The German accommodates itself much less easily to the precision and rapidity of conversation (than the French). By the very nature of its grammatical construction the sense is usually suppressed till the end of the sentence." Mme. de Staël, Germany. Part I, chap. 12. W.

The heaviness of German prose style is a matter of frequent remark. But it is much less owing to the language than to German modes of thought. Few Germans write as they speak; and there is no reason to believe that one who uses French and German with equal fluency will have any more difficulty in expressing his thoughts in the one language than in the other. It is sometimes claimed too that the tendency of modern times is in the direction of the analytic languages like French and English, and away from the synthetic such as German and Russian. It may be said with truth that Modern Greek is more analytic than Ancient, and the descendants of the ancient Latin more so than the parent language. On the other hand, as education becomes general, Greek where it is spoken tends to return to the synthetic type, while next to the English, the German and Russian languages are probably spreading most rapidly. People will always learn those languages that contain information which it is important for them to have. The Germans modelled their written prose after the classic Latin. This led to the extensive use of the periodic construction. In poetic composition it was otherwise, and it is a well-known fact that beginners in German find poetry easier to comprehend than prose. German scholars until recently preferred to use the Latin as the medium for making their thoughts and investigations public to the neglect of their mother tongue. But the classic writers of modern times beginning with Wieland have written prose that is neither heavy nor involved in its construction. Of living writers there is a large proportion who write in a style as clear and straightforward as could be wished. German writers as a class have however been less concerned about the way in which a thought could be most forcibly expressed than about the thought itself. Those who are interested in this matter may find an instructive essay on German style in Professor Hosmer's Short History of German Literature. Professor Hart's German Universities, p. 94 ff., contains some judicious remarks on the same subject. Yet there is a wonderful difference between sentences like those given in the works above named and German of the people as found in books like Grimm's Märchen. The chief reason why classical Latin seems always difficult lies in the fact that hardly any has come down to us as the people spoke. Its remains are always more or less artistic. I cannot help thinking that a language which readily admits the formation of compounds has an important advantage over one which does not, when both are spoken by a people equally civilized.

[18] M. Ad. Regnier, *Traité de la formation des mots dans la langue grecque*, p. 13, gives to the formation of words the name of 'interior syntax.' This is an entirely legitimate extension of the meaning of the word syntax.

[19] The statement that the Latin scarcely allows the formation of compound words is perhaps too strong. We find however as we approach the Augustan age both writers and speakers becoming more and more chary in this respect. Nevertheless a large number of compound words had before this time become thoroughly naturalized and an integral part of the Latin vocabulary. Plautus seems never to have hesitated to form a compound when it suited his purpose, and his writings abound with them. Pacuvius has *repandirostrus, incurvicervicus;* Plautus, *turpilucricupidus.* Others are *coeli-cola, au-spex, mani-pulus, lani-ger, fructi-fer, homi-cida.* The Romance languages like the later Latin do not readily lend themselves to the formation of compounds. The English is much less pliant than its ancestor the Anglo-Saxon. The capacity of the Greek and the German in this respect is almost unlimited. See the 3d vol. of Bopp's Comparative Grammar. Also Tobler, Ztsft. für Völkerpsycho-

logie, Bd. V and VI, 1868 and 1869, and Schroeder, Die formelle Unterscheidung der Redetheile.

[20] It is somewhat difficult to find examples in English to correspond to those here given from the Latin and Greek. We may say "the then king," but we are generally speaking prohibited from putting other words than adjectives between the article and the noun. Somewhat of this nature is the following from Cary's Dante, though it properly is an example of periodic construction,

"me, my wife
Of savage temper, more than aught beside
Hath to this evil brought."

Similarly we find in Acts, "Him, being delivered by the determinate counsel and foreknowledge of God, ye have taken," etc. In German there is hardly any limit to the number of words that may be placed between the article and noun. I have just met the following sentence in a leading Review: "Arbeit eines höchst verdienten und nicht minder thätigen, der Wissenschaft leider im rüstigsten Mannesalter und in voller Kraft entrissenen Forschers," etc. Here *eines* in the first line belongs to *Forschers* in the last.

[21] A number of similar passages occur in Charles Phillips' speech on Napoleon. I give one: "It mattered little whether in the field or in the drawing-room; with the mob or the levée; wearing the jacobin bonnet or the iron crown; banishing a Braganza, or espousing a Hapsburg; dictating peace on a raft to the Czar of Russia, or contemplating defeat at the gallows of Leipzig; he was still the same military despot."

[22] Hermogenes, *de Formis orationis* I, 3. (Walz, Rhetores Graeci, Vol. III, p. 205.) He gives as an example of πλαγιασμὸς the beginning of Herodotus purposely changed: Κροίσου ὄντος Λυδοῦ μὲν γένος, παιδὸς δὲ 'Αλυάττεω, etc. (Chap. 6 begins thus: Κροῖσος ἦν Λυδὸς μὲν γένος, παῖς δὲ 'Αλυάττεω), and as an example of ὀρθότης, the opposite figure 'Εγὼ γὰρ, ὦ 'Άνδρες 'Αθηναῖοι, προσέκρουσα ἀνθρώπῳ πονηρῷ καὶ φιλαπεχθήμονι (Men of Athens, I came in contact with a base and quarrelsome man). That he might leave us in no doubt as to the meaning of πλαγιασμὸς the anonymous author of The Eight Divisions of Rhetoric (Walz, Vol. III, p. 588) says that it is presented in those cases where sentences begin either with a genitive absolute, or a conjunction such as ἐπεί. The reader may further compare a treatise in which are found arranged in alphabetical order the figures cited in the Rhetoric of Hermogenes (Walz, Vol. III, p. 708) and Demetrius, *de Elocutione* (Walz, Vol. IX, p. 564). W.

[23] A detailed examination of Ciceronian periods may be found in Naegelsbach, Lateinische Stylistik § 113. Also in Landgraf's ed. of the Oration pro Sex. Ros. Amer. The periodic construction of sentences seems to be getting more and more uncommon in English. Milton, Hooker, and the older English writers generally used much longer sentences than are now current. The following example is from Milton: "As in a body, when the blood is fresh, the spirits pure and vigorous not only to vital but to rational faculties and those in the acutest and pertest operations of wit and subtilty, it argues in what good plight and constitution the body is, so when the cheerfulness of the people is so sprightly up, as that it has not only wherewith to guard well its own freedom, and safety but to spare, and to bestow upon the solidest and sublimest points of controversy and new

inventions, it betokens us not degenerated, nor drooping to fatal decay, but casting off the old and wrinkled skin of corruption to outlive those pangs and wax young again, entering the glorious ways of truth and prosperous virtue destined to become great and honorable in these latter ages." Here we have two thoughts placed parallel with each other. As ... when ... it argues — so when ... it betokens us ... to outlive. Somewhat similar, but less complex is the following sentence from Beecher: "We did not in the darkest hour believe that God had brought our fathers to this good land to lay the foundation of religious liberty, and wrought such wonders in their preservation, and raised their descendants to such heights of civil and religious liberty, only to reverse the analogy of his providence, and abandon his work." The period is in many cases only an amplification of what our author calls, when speaking of the phrase, the inlocked construction. "But in France, which is destined to refute every object and arrogant doctrine that would limit the human powers, the ardor of a youthful literature has been infused into a nation tending to decline" (Mackintosh). "All this, and the consideration that the daily repeated tone in which a paper publishes or discusses the many occurrences of the day produce a sure effect upon the general tone of the community, ought to warn an editor that if," etc. (Lieber). A writer in No. 23 of the Am. Jour. of Philology points out the fact that in French from the time of Montaigne downward there is a manifest tendency toward shorter sentences. In this author he finds the mean sentence to contain 6.02 verbs, in Fénelon 4.48, in Voltaire 3.89, Daudet 3.38. The same article also dwells on the fact that some French writers for the sake of euphony, emphasis, or piquancy are fond of putting the adjective before the noun instead of in its regular place after it. The tendency toward shorter sentences everywhere so manifest is doubtless owing to the desire on the part of writers to bring their thoughts within the comprehension of as large a number of readers as possible. Even specialists address others besides those who labor in their own department. Comprehension is made easier and knowledge popularized. Men no longer write for the learned or for certain classes, but also for those who are comparatively uneducated. Even those who have large ideas are in a certain sense constrained to cut them up into a number of smaller ones if they would gain a hearing before the public. A most masterly discussion of the styles of three leading modern English prose writers may be found in Minto's Manual of English Prose Literature, republished by Ginn & Co.

CHAPTER III.

THE RELATION BETWEEN THE ORDER OF WORDS AND RHETORICAL EMPHASIS.

We have seen that the order of words is determined by the origin and natural connection of ideas and that the grammatical dependence of the parts of the proposition exercises great influence on this order; yet from this point of view we shall not succeed in adequately explaining all the phenomena which manifest themselves in languages, and particularly in the classical languages. There is another determining cause that is among the most weighty, and one with which we have not as yet concerned ourselves. In order to find this cause the written language is not sufficient: we must have recourse to the spoken and living language. Doubtless some will say that the ancient languages, which are the principal subject of this thesis, speak to us only through the dead letter of their monuments. Besides, when we try to infuse its pristine life into this dead letter the French pronounce differently from the English; these in turn differently from the Germans and Italians, while all probably would be but imperfectly understood by an ancient Roman. We shall therefore leave out of the discussion all that pertains to the pronunciation of consonants and vowels, to long and short quantity.

It behooves us to listen to the ancients who alone are competent judges in this matter, and we shall not be able to add anything to what Cicero, Dionysius of Halicarnassus and the Greek rhetoricians have said upon it. We shall confine ourselves to that part of the pronunciation which pertains mostly to the spirit and the understanding and which for that reason is not subject to so many changes: I mean the rhetorical or oratorical emphasis.

As there is in every word one syllable on which the voice bears more heavily and others over which it glides more lightly, so there is likewise in every proposition a word and in every period a partial proposition, on which the soul and voice bear down with the most energy. This accent is the life-giving principle of speech: the other details of pronunciation are, so to speak, nothing more than its material part. It needs this personal impress, this breath of life, or however we may name it, to give a soul to the vibrations of air which strike our ears. In fact you may read the most admirable writing, utter the freshest and most original thoughts, if you do not indicate by the voice the shades of accentuation, you will not be listened to; your ideas will be regarded as borrowed, hackneyed, though they may have been drawn from the depths of your soul. On the other hand, set off by means of these delicate shadings what may have been said thousands and thousands of times, it will be thought new and found interesting, because your emphasis proves that your words do not proceed merely from your lips but from your soul, from yourself.

The question here mainly is to find out what the influence is that is exercised on the disposition of the parts of the sentence by this vital principle of speech, that is to say, by the emphasis. Albeit, we do not profess to treat in this place of that infinity of shades which the human voice exhibits when expressing anger, love, hate, and all the feelings of the soul. These shades are more easily felt than analyzed: they are to accentuation what colors are to pictures. But there are other differences of emphasis which correspond to light and shade in uncolored designs. It is only the latter that we purpose to consider here, for these alone are determined by the understanding, and may in a given case be demonstrated by the reason, precisely as the effects of light in designs is susceptible of logical explanation from the position of the sun, whereas colors are a matter of taste and sentiment.

The object of this study being thus defined, let us begin with the living languages for which the experience of every day is a sure guide: thence we shall pass to the dead languages which it will be necessary for us to revivify artificially in order to study them in detail.[1]

Ascending accentuation.

The most superficial observer will notice that in French the voice leans by preference and in most cases on the last syllable of words having a masculine termination [2] and on the penultimate of those ending with an *e* mute. In like manner when a proposition is formed of several words the voice ordinarily rises as we advance, so that the last part of the sentence has the strongest and most pronounced emphasis. We see thus that the ascending accentuation prevails in French. This in most cases conforms strictly to the progressive development of the proposition which in French is the descending order of grammatical dependence. For those ideas which syntax subordinates to others, that is, those which serve to restrict a larger idea, having both a more individual character, and being often tacitly placed over against other ideas which they exclude, should in many cases be accented in a more animated and energetic manner. 'A man of courage' (un homme courageux), 'to go in a carriage' (aller en voiture), 'to pursue studies' (faire des études), are phrases in which the sense requires that the dependent ideas, 'courage,' 'carriage,' 'studies,' should be made more prominent by the voice than the ideas upon which they depend, *i.e.*, 'man,' 'to go,' 'to pursue.' It is, in truth, these words which, according to the rules of French grammar, are uttered after those. Ascending accentuation is accordingly often found to be in accord with descending construction.

It must however be admitted that this accentuation or emphasis has come to prevail so entirely in French speech that it is used even in those cases where it seems repugnant to the sense. "It is not the young Horace whose lot we deplore; our pity is aroused by the misfortunes of the old Horace" (Ce n'est pas le jeune Horace dont nous déplorons le sort, notre pitié est excitée par les malheurs du vieil Horace). The contrast between these two persons which we wish to make prominent requires the stress of voice to be on the distinguishing adjectives *young* and *old;* but in reality the voice rises twice on the name of Horace which is given equally to the two persons that are to be particularly distinguished from each other. An attentive listener will find plenty of examples illustrating this stability of the law of accentuation which is closely connected with the regularity of French construction in order to make a more marked contrast with other languages, particularly with the Greek which uses the greatest liberty in the accentuation of the parts of the proposition as well as in their consecution and arrangement. It is difficult to make any positive statements about emphasis in a dead language; there are however certain indications from which we may safely draw conclusions. Nothing is more common in Attic speech than turns like the following: Ὧι ἂν ἀριθμῷ τί ἐγγένηται, περιττὸς ἔσται; (Plato, Phaedo, 105, C.) (If what enters into any number, will it be unequal?) Here we have the interrogative pronoun placed near the middle of the sentence. The sentence from Plato, Ἡ τίσι τί ἀποδιδοῦσα ὀφειλόμενον καὶ προσῆκον τέχνη, ἰατρικὴ καλεῖται; (Republic 332, C.) (The art which gives to whom that which is due and appropriate is called medicine, is it not?) This passage cannot be rendered in French nor in most other languages except by two or three propositions, because it contains two interrogations, one asking about persons, the other about a thing. And further, because the interrogative accent cannot affect one part of the proposition without at the same time taking hold of the others also. We have only interrogative propositions and none that may be interrogative in one part and not in the other or others: we have none that may be doubly or thrice interrogative for the reason that the rigor of our laws of accentuation requires that the impulse of voice which characterizes an interrogation should be communicated only to the beginning of the sentence and never to the middle. The Greeks introduced this impulse where they needed it; they repeated it several times in one and the same sentence, and allowed themselves a freedom in this regard even less restricted than the Romans, who in their turn were more free than the moderns.

There is another phenomenon of the Greek language which seems to have a close connection with this accumulation of interrogatives. I refer now to the accumulated negatives that do not however mutually destroy each other. This might seem very illogical; but it may perhaps be likewise explained as a sort of fresh start which the voice takes at the middle of the proposition. This impulse of the voice may in some sense be said to take the place of a second proposition which another language would make use of. In fact the two phenomena go abreast and mutually explain each other in many instances. Thus the two questions, "Who killed?" and "Who was killed?" can be combined in a single Greek proposition, Τίς τίνα ἐφόνευσεν; the answer may be given in an equally compact phrase, Ὁ Ἀριστογείτων τὸν Ἵππαρχον, and if the reply were negative one might answer after the same analogy, Οὐδεὶς οὐδένα ἐφόνευσεν. We should answer with two separate negative sentences, " Nobody killed, and nobody was killed."

The law of accentuation so fondly cherished by the French language determines very carefully the order which the different complements of the same word shall keep with respect to each other. On this point Beauzée formulated the following rule: " Of several complements belonging to the same word we should put the shortest first and next to the word it qualifies, then the shortest of those which remain, and so on, in order, to the longest which ought to be placed last. By this means those which occupy the last place are as short a distance as possible from the modified term."

The fact is certain, but objection may, I think, be made to the way in which Beauzée explains it. In effect, it seems unworthy of a language so philosophical as the French to be limited by that which is purely external in the signs of thought, that is, by the length of words and by the number of syllables. It is putting the case too strong when he says that grammatical relations lack clearness when an object is separated from its governing verb by twelve letters, but that all is clear when the separation is only by eight letters. Another and more valid objection may be made against this way of stating the case. What would be said if the relation of the different complements were not such as this explanation appears to suppose? Let us take the example cited in the Grammar of Beauzée, " To decorate vice with the externals of virtue" (Parer le vice des dehors de la vertu). The two complements should be placed in this order and not in the reverse order, so that the second may be removed as short a distance as possible from the word *decorate* (parer) upon which the emphasis belongs.

But is it not more natural to regard the second complement as relating not merely to the word *decorate* (parer), but to all that precedes? This word is modified first by its object, *vice* (le vice); and these two terms form therefore one and the same idea, and are qualified in turn by the third term, *with the externals of virtue* (des dehors de la vertu). If we wished to add a fourth, for example, *with the hypocrisy which we cannot too severely stigmatize* (avec cette hypocrisie qu'on ne saurait trop fletrir), this modifying clause would relate not only to *decorate* (parer), but to all that precedes.

When you have linked together two ideas a fusion of them takes place in your mind, — will you proceed to destroy what you have just made, will you again break up this union of ideas in order to attach a third to the first only and then detach this third when there arises the necessity of adding a fourth? This would be performing the labors of Penelope. And what is worse, by all these useless efforts you are trying to break up the unity of the sentence, which can be strongly and satisfactorily established only by combining the ideas that enter into it, as above indicated. Now if the second complement modifies, not the first term, but the two which precede it and which form, apart from the third, an idea that is one and indissoluble, it is evident that there can arise no question of a greater or less distance between words and phrases and their modifiers, because they follow each other without break or interval. An explanation of the order of grammatical complements must then be sought elsewhere, and we believe that we are not mistaken when we claim to have found it in the accentuation. The greater the number of men or resources under your control, the greater is your power. In like manner the accent of a syllable is strong in proportion to the number of less accented syllables that surround it, — for it cannot be said of any syllable of a word that it has no accent. In pronouncing successively the two terms *vice* and *the externals of virtue* the voice will of its own accord rise more on the word 'virtue' than on the word 'vice' for the reason that there are fewer subordinate words and syllables that serve to bring out the accent in the one case than in the other. The deeper the shadow, the more need there is of light. Owing to the ascending accentuation of the French language we should place the longest modifier next after the shortest and say, "To decorate vice with the externals of virtue" (Parer le vice des dehors de la vertu). But if you should wish to pronounce with the ascending accentuation, "To decorate with the externals of virtue, vice" (Parer des dehors de la vertu, le vice), it would require an effort to place the stress of voice on the second modifier, which is comparatively short, after the first, which is much longer. It is this which affects the hearer unpleasantly.

This disagreeable impression is the result of a sort of violence done to the usual pronunciation, yet it can in certain cases be employed with great effect when our object is to impress vividly our auditor; to bring into marked prominence an idea with more than ordinary force. Upon such a supposition the sentence we have just condemned may even be defended. It might be allowable to say, "Great God, you dare to decorate with the externals of virtue, vice" (Grand Dieu! vous osez parer des dehors de la vertu, le vice), if the speaker's intention was to give vent to a violent burst of indignation. Thus we read in Bossuet: "She was constrained to appear in society and to parade, so to speak, in the Louvre, where she was born with so much glory, *all the magnitude of her misery*" (Elle fût contrainte de paraitre au monde et d'etaler, pour ainsi dire, au Louvre, où elle était née avec tant de gloire, toute l'étendue de sa misère). "God kept twelve years without respite, without any consolation from men, *our unhappy queen* (let us proudly give her this title), of which she has made a matter of thanksgiving" (Dieu a tenu douze ans sans relâche, sans aucune consolation de la part des hommes, notre malheureuse reine (donnons-lui hautement ce titre), dont elle a fait un sujet d'actions de grâces).

In this case the intensity of the accent is more remarked because it is less supported by subordinate syllables: we are the more vividly impressed because the effect seems out of proportion to its cause.

After attempting another explanation of the rule which determines the order of complements let us return to this one whose formula, it is true, does not appear quite sufficient in all respects. If there are several modifiers of the same word let us arrange them by reason of their length beginning with the shortest and ending with the longest. So says the rule. It has been deduced from an incontestable fact, it is confirmed by good authors. It has been deduced by analysis and decomposition, as all good rules of grammar should be, after the true method in physics. It has been found by investigation and comparison that such was the usage, I might almost say, instinctively, of good authors and persons who speak the language well. Grammar came afterward and said: Since men speak thus habitually one should speak so because it is grammatical; and henceforth this will be law. But a rule discovered by decomposition ought to be reversed, if one wants to make it a rule of composition. The method of establishing the law ought to have no influence on the mode of expressing it. Without that it would be formulated inversely. I will explain my meaning by an example.

Beauzée finds fault with this sentence of La Bruyère: "Who has not sometimes in his hands a libertine to subdue, and lead back by gentle and insinuating conversations to docility" (Qui n'a pas quelquefois sous sa main un libertin à réduire, et à ramener par de douces et insinuantes conversations à la docilité). The author of the *Characters* ought to have said, according to the grammarian, "to docility by gentle and insinuating conversations." But this modifier which expresses the means of conversion is secondary in the thought of the author. He has only added it *en passant;* and for this reason while preferring a less harmonious but more correct order he has not assigned to it the last place. If we wished to correct this sentence in order to make it more elegant it would be proper not to displace the ideas, but to give greater extent to the complement, which wounds the ear by its brevity. We might say, for example, "To lead back by gentle and insinuating conversations to the docility of reasonable minds which is far removed from the indolence of feeble minds."

This example shows that the rule of the grammarians ought to be reversed. Instead of saying, "Of several complements belonging to the same word we should put the shortest first and next to the word to which it belongs, then the shortest of those that remain, and so on, in order, to the longest which ought to be placed last," we should rather say, "Of several complements relating to the same word give the most concise form to that which immediately follows the modified word, and, as you go on, give to the modifying terms a fuller and more extended form." Speech is the servant of thought, and not thought the servant of speech. For this reason a rule which recasts a sentence to make it conform to the accentuation required by the thought, seems more worthy of the French language than one which, by changing the order and importance of ideas to suit the syllables, makes the thought conform to the fortuitous length of words. A long word does not necessarily embody a great thought. In this sentence of Bossuet, "Henrietta was destined, first by her illustrious birth and next by her unfortunate captivity, to error and heresy" (Henriette était destinée, premièrement par sa glorieuse naissance, et ensuite par sa malheureuse captivité, à l'erreur et à l'hérésie), the modifier at the end of the sentence is made up of two almost synonymous terms. Why? Because it is placed after two others of considerable length, and of greater importance to the sense.

According to the rule of the grammarians the great orator ought to have constructed his sentence so as to read, "Henrietta was destined to heresy, first, by her illustrious birth," etc.; but with this displacement of words he would likewise have displaced the climax of his thought. For the same reason he says, "How many poor subsisted during the whole course of her life by the boundless profusion of her alms" (Que de pauvres ont subsisté pendant tout le cours de sa vie par l'immense profusion de ses aumônes), and not "by her alms during the whole course of her life." It is, further, for the same reason that he says, "You have exposed, in the midst of the greatest dangers of war, a life so precious and so indispensable as yours" (Vous avez exposé au milieu des plus grands hazards de la guerre une vie aussi précieuse et aussi nécessaire que le vôtre), and not "a life so precious in the midst of the," etc.

Descending accentuation.

The law of ascending accentuation exists more or less in other languages besides the French, and appears to be founded on this sentiment natural to man, which makes him take pleasure in progress, in growth; and because he has an inborn distaste for decrease, for retrograde movement. In truth, a pronunciation which should continue to grow feebler from the first word of the proposition to the last, would end by going to sleep; but we are aroused by an accentuation which keeps rising and becoming stronger. Men have sometimes amused themselves by making verses in which the first word is a monosyllable, the second a dissyllable, and so on with an ascending progression. These verses are in the form of a club and are hence called *versus rhopalici; Rem tibi concessi, doctissime, dulcisonoram*. After what we have just said on the relation existing between the length of terms and the force of the accent or emphasis, there is in such verses not only progression in the number of syllables, but also in the stress with which the words are pronounced. For this reason they have an agreeable sound. But construct them so that the number of syllables will decrease from word to word and they will be insupportable.

And yet this descending accentuation which is in so high a degree unpleasant when dominant in discourse, becomes not only bearable but even agreeable when, by intermingling it with the ascending, its disagreeable monotony is relieved. From this point of view I believe the following classification can be established. The French language is almost entirely under the domination of the ascending accentuation while the classic languages are fond of interrupting the advancing movement which it represents and of spreading over the picture of discourse a great variety of lights and shadows.[3]

In the first place the harshness of the ascending accentuation in the Greek and Latin languages is often mitigated, especially at the end of periods of considerable length which serve to conclude the development of a thought and to crown, so to speak, an oratorical *morceau*. We may often notice that after the most significant words, those upon which the voice leans most heavily, there follow yet two or three words which though completing the grammatical construction, of which they form as it were the pivotal points, they add but little to the sense and contain no ideas essential thereto. It is by these words which furnish no material for thought or imagination, but which are necessary to fill out the grammatical scheme, that the voice descends to its proper level. These words form what has been felicitously called the cadence of the sentence. Examples are abundant. It is in this way that Cicero closes the oration *pro lege Manilia*. *Sed ego me hoc honore praeditum, tantis vestris beneficiis affectum, statui, Quirites, vestram voluntatem et rei publicae dignitatem et salutem provinciarum atque sociorum meis omnibus commodis atque rationibus* PRAEFERRE *oportere* (But it has seemed to me that I, invested with my present honors and graced with so many kind offices on your part, ought to prefer your wishes and the dignity of the republic and the safety of our provinces and allies, to all considerations of my own private interest).

In like manner we have at the beginning of Chap. XVI: *Potestis igitur jam constituere, Quirites, hanc auctoritatem, multis postea rebus gestis magnisque vestris judiciis amplificatam, quantum apud exteras nationes* VALITURAM *esse existimetis* (You are able accordingly now, O Romans, to estimate accurately how much weight this authority of his — especially since it has been further increased by many subsequent exploits and by many commendatory resolutions of your own — will have with those kings and among foreign nations).

At the end of Chap. XIV occurs this passage: *Et quisquam dubitavit, quin huic tantum bellum transmittendum sit, qui ad omnia nostrae memoriae bella conficienda divino quodam consilio* NATUS *esse videatur*. The words printed in small capitals are the last whose meaning will bear a strong emphasis. *Oportere, esse existimetis*, finally *esse videatur*, two words that often serve as a close in Cicero's periods, are necessary to the complete grammatical construction, but they do not, strictly speaking, add anything to the thought. It is while uttering them that the voice descends harmoniously from its elevation. They are, as it were, the last tinklings of a bell that are borne to our ears, which we love to hear after the hour has struck. It is well known with what art the ancient orators placed and measured their closes, and that they studied them all the more conscientiously because they felt that these vocal utterances being destitute of ideas, they must need attach greater importance to their corporal and sensible parts than was the case with significant terms. The minute directions of Aristotle, Theophrastus, Cicero and others as to the rhythm and feet with which periods should close are evidence of this fact.

Let us hasten to put by the side of these periods some examples in which the emphasis continues to rise to the end. We shall take them from Chap. V of the same oration. *Legati quod erant appellati superbius, Corinthum patres vestri, tŏtius Graeciae lumen, extinctum esse voluerunt; vos eum regem inultum esse patiemini, qui legatum populi romani consularem vinculis ac verberibus atque omni supplicio excruciatum* NECAVIT? *Illi libertatem civium romanorum imminutam non tulerunt; vos vitam ereptam esse* NEGLIGETIS? *Jus legationis verbo violatum illi persecuti sunt; vos legatum, omni supplicio interfectum,* RELINQUETIS (Because their embassadors had been haughtily spoken to, your ancestors determined that Corinth the *light* of all Greece should be *blotted* out. Will *you* allow *that* king to remain unpunished who has murdered a lieutenant of the Roman people of consular rank after torturing him with chains and scourging and every sort of punishment? *They* would not endure the freedom of the Roman people to be diminished; will *you* be indifferent when their lives are taken? They avenged the privileges of our embassy when violated by a word; will you abandon an embassador who has been put to death with every cruelty?). One needs only to read these sentences to feel that which is characteristic of them and which is perfectly expressed in the emphasis that is not weakened by a cadence but keeps on getting more intense to the last word.[4] In these vigorous phrases you see the orator in the attack, you see him constraining the will of his hearers: they are, to use the figure of Quintilian, like arrows, and their sharp points bury themselves in the soul of the hearer. If we examine them more closely we shall find that each of the three periods is composed of two parts, but it is only the second which terminates in this violent manner. The first, which occupies its place only to make a contrast with the second and to heighten its energy, has a more regular and tranquil march and terminates with a harmonious subsidence of the oratorical emphasis. Let us add some examples from the Greek. Demosthenes in one of his admirable comparisons uses this well rounded and harmonious form of expression:

Ὥσπερ γὰρ οἰκίας, οἶμαι, καὶ πλοίου καὶ τῶν ἄλλων τῶν τὰ κάτωθεν ἰσχυρότατ᾽ εἶναι δεῖ, οὕτω καὶ τῶν πράξεων τὰς ἀρχὰς καὶ τὰς ὑποθέσεις, ἀληθεῖς καὶ δικαίας εἶναι προσήκει (Just as, I think, the lowest parts of a house and a ship and other like things need to be the strongest, so likewise the foundations and first principles of actions ought to be true and just). It may be remarked that the cadence εἶναι προσήκει like *esse videatur* does not sink directly but rises a little toward the end, thus making it finer and more stately. But when the orator castigates the apathy of the Athenians his period ends with a harsh emphasis: Οὐ δὴ θαυμαντόν ἐστιν εἰ στρατευόμενος καὶ πονῶν ἐκεῖνος αὐτὸς καὶ παρὼν ἐφ᾽ ἅπασι καὶ μηδένα καιρὸν μηδ᾽ ὥραν παραλείπων ἡμῶν μελλόντων καὶ ψηφιζομένων καὶ πυνθανομένων περιγίγνεται (Verily, it is not surprising if that man, by leading his army in person, by enduring hardship with them, by being everywhere present himself and neglecting no occasion nor season, gets the better of us who are everlastingly getting ready and voting decrees and making inquiries).

I would designate these two kinds of periods as periods with masculine terminations and periods with feminine terminations, because they produce an effect analogous to that of masculine and feminine rhymes. In fact this terminology owes its existence to the circumstance that most of the adjectives are accented on the final syllable in the masculine and on the penult in the feminine gender. In the sixteenth century the *e* when silent was called the feminine *e*. Besides one perceives just as in these periods that there is something virile and vigorous in masculine rhymes, and something gentle and tender in feminine rhymes.[5] Might one not be justified in claiming to find a symbolic expression of these shades of character in the very formation of the genders of the adjective? Might not the weakening of the final *a* of the Latin, the apocope of the final syllable *us*, so common in the French language, have been caused by a sort of impalpable feeling of these shades of difference? *Bonus bon bonne, divinus divin divine, generosus généreux généreuse*. One cannot hear these words pronounced, though one may not know their meaning, without feeling an indefinable something virile in their sound that suddenly darts forth and then stops abruptly. That cadence, on the contrary, which gradually retards the movement, has a more gentle, one might almost say effeminate, character. The poetry of antiquity also affords some analogies in the various cæsuras that are designated as masculine and feminine.

We have thus had an example of the descending accentuation; but there is another, more important and more extensive in its application. When the imagination is vividly impressed by an idea, or even when a sentiment that is stronger than the man who entertains it, escapes him almost in spite of himself, the most expressive term and fullest of that which occupies his soul, ordinarily the goal of the discourse (see Chap. I), is put at the beginning of the sentence, and on this the greatest stress of voice. Scævola when disclosing to Pyrrhus who the strange man is that dares defy the king even in his own tent, says to him, ROMANUS *civis sum* (Livy II, 12). The whole force of the disclosure lies in the first word. Without premeditation, without preamble, this word *Roman* suddenly illumines this unknown person and this incomprehensible action. The other two words are added merely to complete the construction. Besides, the ancient languages frequently use this vivid and pathetic emphasis where the circumstances are not so startling. In the Apology, Socrates represents himself as addressed with this remark, " This man does not believe in the divinity of the sun, because he claims that it is a stone." Ἀναξαγόρου οἴει κατηγορεῖν, replies he, Do you think you are accusing Anaxagoras? By the sole name of Anaxagoras, which is placed first, Socrates shows the entire insincerity of his accusers. Let us add another example of the emphasis which naturally attaches to the first word of a sentence and raises it above others. Lysias in his judicial harangues often addresses himself to the witnesses, requesting them to corroborate what he says. The following form of expression is very frequent: καὶ κάλει μοι τοὺς μάρτυρας, καὶ μοι ἀνάβητε τούτων μάρτυρες. The main idea μάρτυρες is thrown to the end of the sentence — the accentuation is ascending. In a single instance (Contra Agor. § 66) the orator uses this form, Ὡς δ' ἀληθῆ λέγω, μάρτυρας κάλει, but a little farther along he returns to the usual order. What is the motive of this exception, which is the less to be attributed to chance as the formula has the sanction of very frequent usage? Lysias is accusing Agoratus. He lays to his charge all imaginable crimes against the state; he caps the climax by accusing him of crimes against persons. He reproaches him with being an adulterer, rapidly but with intense exasperation. For this reason he omits the articles and pronouns which he usually employs in this formula. For the same reason too the principal word, witnesses, comes first to his mind and is uttered forthwith. "Call" is therefore a word of only secondary importance. One step further, a little more impetuosity and the orator would have cut off this word altogether and concentrated his whole thought in the one energetic exclamation μάρτυρας.

The examples of a purely descending accentuation or emphasis that we have given fall within a circle of two or three words; nor do we believe it would be easy to find any of greater extent. A descending accentuation which should extend over a longer sentence would be disagreeable. It is natural to require that the voice should recover itself: and this is exactly what we see taking place in the ancients. They furnish us with many sentences, and among them some of their finest, of which the emphasis is divided between the first and last word.[6]

These two accents have not however the same value: that of the beginning is, so to speak, the spontaneous accent, that of the end the reflective accent. These differences, nevertheless, are no reason for saying that the orators failed to recognize their effect and likewise to calculate the place of the one as well as the other. Nature has sometimes the effect of art. We hasten to add here some examples. Demosthenes, recalling the days of consternation which preceded the battle of Chaeronea, those days in which a man was eagerly sought who should give counsels worthy of his native land, Demosthenes cries out, Ἐφάνην τοίνυν οὗτος ἐν ἐκείνῃ τῇ ἡμέρᾳ ἐγώ (Now there appeared the needed man on that day, and it was I). What I should like to call the illumination of the emphasis spreads itself over the words Ἐφάνην and ἐγώ, which are placed in relief at the beginning and end of the sentence; the rest is placed in the shadow. The former has, as it were, escaped in the eagerness that hurries the orator along, and this verb does in reality bear in its termination the secret of the sentence, the ἐγώ which the speaker sees from the beginning but which he kept back, kept waiting in order to hurl it with greater *éclat* into the midst of his auditors.

There is a similar arrangement in another place in the same chapter. Πολλάκις δὲ τοῦ κήρυκος ἐρωτῶντος, ἀνίστατ' οὐδείς ('Though the crier often repeated the invitation (to speak), no one rose). All the energy of the accentuation is concentrated in the words πολλάκις and οὐδείς.[7] It is not necessary to lean on the two verbs because they are already in the sentence just preceding and are no longer of much importance. In order to get examples from the Latin we need only recall these well-known passages from Cicero: PATERE *tua consilia* NON SENTIS? CONSTRICTAM *jam horum omnium conscientia teneri conjurationem tuam* NON VIDES? *Ad* MORTEM *te, Catilina, duci jussu consulis* JAMPRIDEM *oportebat.* LUGET *senatus,* MOERET *equester ordo, tota civitas confecta* SENIO *est;* SQUALENT *municipia,* AFFLICTANTUR *coloniae, agri denique ipsi tam beneficum, tam salutarem, tam* MANSUETAM *civem* DESIDERANT. This last example shows that a purely descending accent is suited only to very short sentences. Twice do incidental sentences fall into the descending movement, but the more extended ones are plainly animated by the contrary movement. This disposition of words recalls the precept given by the masters of the oratorical art, and among others by Quintilian. He advises the placing of the most weighty arguments at the beginning and end of the sentence and the weaker ones in the middle. We have then the same principle applied to the composition of a discourse and the arrangement of a sentence. The most important places are the beginning and the end; they are, so to speak, the places of honor both in the order of arguments and in the order of words.

The repose of emphasis.

When sentences are of somewhat greater extent it is evident that the positions at the beginning and end of the sentence are not sufficient to contain the emphasized words; the ebb and flow of the voice needs also to be felt at the middle of the sentence either by secondary or primary emphasis. It is true that the same sentence may convey different meanings, according as the emphasis is placed on certain words or on others; the sense must decide, and the arrangement of the words is not an unerring guide. The ancients however liked to dispose their words in such a way that the emphasis required by the sense to be on certain words should also be in harmony with the disposition of the words and should grow out of that disposition, so to speak, spontaneously. A change of accent or emphasis usually carried along with it a change in the order of words, the order of words in turn often indicating to us the emphasis which the author had in mind. There is a mutual correspondence between these two facts. The great perfection of the ancient orators consists partly in the art with which they disposed their verbal material so as to make emphasis and correct expression stand out prominently of their own accord. Yet while the orators have given to this art the highest development, it is found more or less in all authors and in all languages: it is in the *genius* of the ancients, or as some would rather say, in the *genius* of their languages. In fact, if there is an art in which they excelled it is assuredly that of giving a soul to verbal expression. But we must pass from these general considerations to the details of our subject.

We have seen that the places at the beginning and end of sentences, that is, after or before a repose of voice, are the most appropriate for emphasized words. We have seen also that the accent of a word or syllable is strong in direct ratio to the number of words or syllables over which its influence extends. The ancients did no more than apply these principles in the artificial arrangement of their words into sentences. If it is necessary to strongly emphasize a word, place near it another on which the sense does not require you to put any emphasis. Thus the emphatic word, even when placed neither at the beginning nor at the end of the sentence, will have an advantageous position, for the emphasis is enhanced by the repose of emphasis that accompanies it. There are words which do not express ideas but only the relation of ideas: they are, to use a term of Chinese grammar, the *empty words* of discourse. By bringing these into relation with *full words*, that is, words expressing ideas, you will have placed near the latter not only a repose of emphasis, but a repose of idea, thereby adding to the energy of its emphasis. Plato, in the Apology of Socrates (19 E), passes in review the principal sophists who in his time made a display of their wisdom for pay. He names Gorgias, Prodicus, and Hippias, but he wants to attach an ironical importance to the name of the latter. In order to do so he makes use of a device which could not be imitated in most other languages with the same nicety: he simply adds a little particle to the name of Hippias. This is the passage: Ὥσπερ Γοργίας τε ὁ Λεοντῖνος καὶ Πρόδικος ὁ Κεῖος καὶ Ἱππίας δὲ ὁ Ἡλεῖος. The force of this particle needs to be carefully pointed out. Its principal office is to produce a repose of thought and of emphasis, and thus to enhance the value of the emphasis of the preceding word. "And Hippias too." The words 'chiefly,' 'especially,' and others of like signification, have a too clearly defined meaning to render the shade of thought expressed by δέ.[8] The delicacy of this shade is chiefly owing to the fact that the Greek particle acts less through the idea that it calls up than through the repose of idea which it causes. We find in the Meno (87 E) a similar example where the author has used the stronger form δή. He says, Ὑγιεία, φαμὲν, καὶ ἰσχὺς καὶ κάλλος καὶ πλοῦτος δή. Many more examples are given in the Grammar of Professor Kühner. In the following passage the particle δὲ is placed with great force in the very middle of a term that is almost indivisible: Καὶ οἵ τε ἄλλοι προθύμως τῷ Τελευτίᾳ ὑπήρετουν ... καὶ ἡ τῶν Θηβαίων δὲ πόλις (Hell. V, 2, 37). (The others were zealously serving Teleutias, and the city of the Thebans particularly.) The particle γε is often used in the same way. Let us cite but a single passage in which it serves to exhibit the delicate irony of Plato: Ἀλλὰ, μέντοι, ἦν δ' ἐγώ, Σιμονίδῃ γε οὐ ῥᾴδιον ἀπιστεῖν (Whatever one may think of other people, he can't well help believing Simonides). The same enclitic is repeated with great emphasis by Polynices in Sophocles when he addresses this touching prayer to his sisters (Oed. Col. 1405):

Ὦ τοῦδ' ὅμαιμοι παῖδες, ἀλλ' ὑμεῖς, ἐπεὶ
Τὰ σκληρὰ πατρὸς κλύετε τοῦδ' ἀρωμένου,
Μήτοι με πρὸς θεῶν σφώ γ', ἐὰν γ' αἱ τοῦδ' ἀραὶ
Πατρὸς τελῶνται, ... μη μ' ἀτιμάσῃ τέ γε ...

(Oh sisters sprung from the same blood with me, but ye, since ye hear our father imprecating these awful curses, do not ye at least, by the gods, if the curses of this my father be accomplished, do not treat me with dishonor). It is well known that the particle ἄν is placed by preference after the word to which the writer wishes to call particular attention by emphasis; sometimes it seems to be even unnecessarily repeated, but it serves to draw special attention to several words of the sentence. Oedipus incensed by the obstinate refusal of Teiresias, cries (Oed. Tyr. 339, 340), Τίς γὰρ τοιαῦτ' ἄν οὐκ ἄν ὀργίζοιτ' ἔπη κλύων; (*Who* would *not* be angered upon hearing *such* words?) The repose of idea or thought afforded by γὰρ and the repetition of ἄν give a certain energy to the three ideas, τίς, τοιαῦτα and οὐ. Another verse of Sophocles which contains three ἄν among nine words is the following, Πῶς ἄν οὐκ ἄν ἐν δίκῃ θάνοιμ' ἄν; (How should I not justly die?) In the following passage the particle καὶ is repeated three times, and its force is exerted, not on the word that follows, but on that which precedes: Ἵνα καὶ ἴδῃς ὅσα καὶ εἴδη ἔχει ἡ κακία, ἅ γε δὴ καὶ ἄξια θέας (In order that you may also see how many forms vice has, so far at least as they are worth seeing). At least this is the explanation I would give of the apparent transposition of this particle. Sometimes we find it placed before a word with which it does not seem directly connected; in such cases its sole use is to bring this word into prominence. For example, καὶ τοῦτο μὲν ἧττον καὶ θαυμαστόν in place of καὶ ἧττον θαυμαστόν (Plato, Symp. 177 B). Ταῦτα γὰρ μᾶλλον καὶ ἐξαπατᾶν δύναται τοὺς ἐναντίους (Xen. Cyrop. I, 6, 38).

It will thus be seen that these little words enhance the terms near which they are placed, not by any meaning that is peculiar to them, but solely by the repose of emphasis which they cause. All particles whatever be their function elsewhere, be it restrictive like γε, or conditional like ἄν, or causative like γὰρ, produce the same effect. The indeterminate adjective τι the signification of which certainly does not contain a shadow of gradation or opposition, is employed exactly like δὲ and δὴ in the passages from Plato cited below. We have before us a case of enumeration: Εἰ μὲν τις φρούριον τι πρόυδωκεν ἤ ναῦν ἤ στρατόπεδόν τι. Of what use is the repeated τι, if not to give greater emphasis to στρατόπεδον? But let us allow the orator (Lysias, Accus. Philo. 26) to go on with his sentence, ἐν ᾧ μέρος τι ἐτύγχανεν τῶν πολιτῶν ὄν. The word μέρος is separated by two words from the genitive on which it depends, and they are words which have no important nor oratorical emphasis. Why? A portion of the citizens is opposed by the whole city, μέρος τῶν πολιτῶν and ὅλη ἡ πόλις; the arrangement of the words takes the place of μόνον. Let us go on: ταῖς ἐσχάταις ἄν ζημίαις ἐζημιοῦτο. Here we have again the particle ἄν placed, not next to the verb to which it relates, but near the pathetic adjective. The whole passage reads, ἄξιον δὲ καὶ τόδε ἐνθυμηθῆναι, ὅτι εἰ μέν τις φρούριόν τι προὔδωκεν ἢ ναῦν ἢ στρατόπεδόν τι, ἐν ᾧ μέρος τι ἐτύγχανε τῶν πολιτῶν ὄν, ταῖς ἐσχάταις ἄν ἐζημιοῦτο, οὗτος δὲ προδοὺς ὅλην τὴν πόλιν οὐχ ὅπως τιμωρηθήσεται παρασκευάζεται (It is well to remember that if any one had betrayed a ship or an army however small, he would have suffered the death penalty, but this fellow after betraying a whole city, etc.).

The harangue from which the last extract has been made furnishes, some lines further on, an example of a particle whose emphasis is enhanced by two other particles surrounding it. Τίς γὰρ ἄν ποτε ῥήτωρ ἐνεθυμήθη . . . (What orator would ever have imagined). Here Lysias in order to point out the impossibility of such a supposition, leans on the conditional particle which corresponds very nearly to the expression *would have been able* (aurait pu) of the English, and in order to detach this particle from every term of greater importance which might weaken it, he places it between two other particles pronounced without support. This artificial arrangement which produces a pleasing effect for the full words (signs of ideas) appears to be necessary to attract the emphasis upon particles that are habitually pronounced lightly.

This interruption which gives more energy to the adjoining words is often produced with even greater effect by certain words and phrases that form a brief parenthesis in the middle of the sentence. Of this kind are οἶμαι, ἔμοιγε δοκεῖν, ὦ ἄνδρες Ἀθηναῖοι, ἔφη, and many other short phrases interjected between words, breaking their continuity but bringing into prominence their emphasis, Εἰς δέ γε, οἶμαι, τὰς ἄλλας περιόντες πόλεις . . . εἰς τυραννίδας ἕλκουσι τὰς πολιτείας. Tragic poets, says Plato (Rep. 568 C), shall be excluded from our commonwealth: let them go and mislead other cities. The author wishing to bring the word *other* into prominence has placed before it, not counting the article and the preposition, two particles and one of the short parenthetic words named above, while close after it he has put a participle which separates it from its substantive. Πόθεν οὖν, ἔφη, ὦ Σώκρατες, τῶν τοιούτων ἀγαθὸν ἐπῳδὸν ληψόμεθα, ἐπειδὴ, σύ, ἔφη, ἡμᾶς ἀπολείπεις; (Plat. Phaedo, 78 A) (And where shall we find a good charmer, Sokrates, he asked, now that you are leaving us?) It was of no use to repeat ἔφη unless it was intended to give a more intense emphasis to the pronoun σύ. PARVA *inquis, res est. A* PHILOSOPHIS, *inquis, ista sumis.* TRIUMPHABAT, *quid quaeris, Hortensius* (Cic. Paradox, chap. II; Ad Attic. I, 16).

The particles being the lightest elements of the sentence one need be little surprised that the ancients transposed and even repeated them at their pleasure in order to produce certain effects of accent and emphasis. The same thing may be said of the parenthetic words and phrases of which we have just spoken. But the ancients went even farther in this direction. They transposed all the parts of the sentence; they arranged the verbs, substantives and all the constituent elements of speech solely to produce these effects. In all that we say there are certain words that embody thoughts, and there are others of a parasitic nature that we add because we are compelled to do so by the nature of spoken language; for in order to be clear we must conform to a certain scheme or framework established by usage. These latter words are what I think may be properly designated as the fillings of the sentence. The energy of the thought is enfeebled; but such is the necessity imposed by the essential difference between thought and speech that even the most concise writers are constrained by it. They could not ignore it if they would. The secondary terms obscure the principal ones, yet one dares not ignore them. This is an obstacle which seems insurmountable, and yet the ancients have shown that they know how to overcome it or even turn it into an advantage. They had the skill to use what must almost of necessity attenuate the thought, in such a way as to reinforce its energy. They achieved these admirable results by the tact they displayed in disposing all the elements of the sentence. It is thus that they have shown themselves the true artists of speech.

Some one, for example, is relating a general's feats of arms. Clearness requires that the same proper name should be often repeated, but elegance requires its suppression: place it therefore under the shadow, so to speak, of other words more strongly emphasized. This is what Xenophon has done, first for Thimbron, then for Dercyllides, in the third book of his Hellenics. Καὶ σὺν μὲν ταύτῃ τῇ στρατιᾷ, ὁρῶν Θίμβρων τὸ ἱππικὸν, ἐς τὸ πεδίον οὐ κατέβαινεν (chap. 5). We glide over the proper name because we are looking for the object of the participle ὁρῶν. Ἦν δὲ ἅς (πόλεις) ἀσθενεῖς οὔσας καὶ κατὰ κράτος ὁ Θίμβρων ἐλάμβανον (chap. 7). Ἦν δὲ καὶ πρόσθεν ὁ Δερκιλλίδας πολέμιος τῷ Φαρναβάζῳ (chap. 9). Ὡς δὲ ταῦτα ἐγένετο, ἐλθὼν ὁ Δερκιλλίδας ἐς τὴν Βιθυνίδα Θρᾴκην ἐκεῖ διεχείμαζεν. Καὶ τὰ μὲν ἄλλα ὁ Δερκιλλίδας ἀσφαλῶς φέρων καὶ ἄγων τὴν Βιθυνίδα διετέλει (Bk. III, 2, 2). It would hardly be possible in a modern language to find a place for these nouns where their repetition in a sentence would be so little unpleasant to the ear as in Greek.

There are words that signify but little and manifest a disposition to retire within the recesses of the sentence. Of this number is the participle ἔχων which by losing its verbal value often becomes little more than a preposition. It sometimes precedes its object just like the prepositions; but sometimes — and it would seem that this disposition of it is the most elegant — it is so inlocked among other more important words that it is hardly noticed in the pronunciation. Τοὺς δὲ ἀπὸ Φρυγίας τῆς παρ' Ἑλλησπόντον συμβαλεῖν φασὶ Γαβαῖον ἔχοντα εἰς Καΰστρου πεδίον (Xen. Cyr. II, 1, 5). (But the dwellers in Phrygia on the Hellespont, they say that G. will collect into, etc.) Σώματα μὲν ἔχοντες ἀνδρῶν ἥκετε οὐ μεμπτά (ib. 11). (The bodies of these men are irreproachable, but their arms and equipments may need attention.) Ἑπτακοσίους ἔχων ὁπλίτας, ναῦς ἔχων ἐβδομήκοντα, κτλ.

Words on the contrary have an intensity of signification which is expressed by emphasis and by the choice of a suitable place in the sentence for this emphasis. Ὁρᾶτε γάρ ... οἷ προελήλυθεν ἀσελγείας ἄνθρωπος (You see to what a height of insolence this man has advanced).

Here the pronoun οἶ expresses the idea of an extraordinary degree: for this reason it is detached from the genitive which defines it and followed by a verb of comparatively little importance, by which arrangement the emphasis on the pronoun is increased. Νῦν δ' εἰς τοῖθ' ἥκει τὰ πράγματα αἰσχύνης (But now our affairs are come to such a condition of disgrace).

Here τοῦθ'... αἰσχύνης have the same relation to each other and the same arrangement with οἶ... ἀσελγείας above. *Ad* HANC *te amentiam natura peperit* (Cic. Cat. I, 10). QUAS *ego pugnas et quantas strages edidi* (Cic. Ad Attic. I, 16).

Generally speaking, feeble words — by which we mean such words as would render the delivery of a sentence languid — if they occupy a prominent place in the sentence, are concealed by their position near a striking word which they serve in turn to make still more conspicuous. *Quod indicat non ingratam negligentiam* DE RE *hominis magis quam de verbis laborantis* (Cic. Orat. 23). Here *hominis laborantis* would naturally be put next to *negligentiam* which they limit, and *magis* be placed with the participle. *Et sibi et aliis persuaserat* NULLIS *illum judicibus effugere posse* (Cic. Ad Attic. I, 16). He (Hortensius) had persuaded both himself and others that he (illum, Clodium) could, etc. Ὅσῳ ἂν πλειόνων ἐάσω μεν ἐκεῖνον γενέσθαι κύριον, τοσούτῳ χαλεπωτέρῳ καὶ ἰσχυροτέρῳ χρησόμεθα ἐχθρῷ (Dem. de Chersoneso, p. 102). Here the emphatic positions are occupied by κύριον and ἐχθρῷ. Σωφρονέστερον γάρ ἐστιν ὕστερον πᾶσι τῶν ἔργων τὰς χάριτας ἀποδιδόναι (Lysias, Acc. Philonis, § 24). Here ἐστιν is of comparatively little importance and πᾶσι could easily be omitted altogether; it is here only to make ὕστερον more conspicuous. We notice a tendency in these passages to make the words that receive the oratorical emphasis alternate with feebler words and thus produce a sort of rhythmic movement. This rhythm appertains not to the syllables but to the words themselves that may be considered as forming in their totality either strong or weak tenses. By this rhythm I would explain the frequent hyperbatons in Plato. Ὑβριστὴς εἶ, ἔφη, Σώκρατες, ὁ Ἀγάθων (Symp. 175 E). Ἀληθέστατα, ἔφη, λέγεις, ὁ Κέβης, ὦ Σώκρατες (Phaedo, 83 E). This arrangement though it may appear altogether artificial was doubtless entirely natural to the Athenians, otherwise

Plato would not have used it in the familiar conversations of his dialogues.

In the examples drawn from Lysias two of these strong tenses — if I may use this term in a slightly modified sense — are brought closer together than the remaining strong tenses of the sentence. The sense requires the substantives ἔργων and χάριτας above to be pronounced with energy: they are therefore separated by the article only. In § 21 of the same oration we find 'Ἀντιφάνει δὲ οὐδὲν προσήκουσα πιστεύσασα ἔδωκεν εἰς τὴν ἑαυτῆς ταφὴν τρεῖς μνᾶς ἀργυρίου. The two participles in the sentence are of equal importance, need to be equally emphasized and are placed close together so that they may, in a certain sense, collide. The author has still further enhanced the contrast by using words with assonant terminations. Some editors disagreeably affected by this cacophony propose to read προσήκοντι; but I believe that what in every other case would be a blemish adds a beauty to this passage. The contrast made evident by the juxtaposition of the two words is made more effective by the similarity of their form. In order to make prominent the essential difference of two objects it must be disengaged from all accidental diversities by making the objects equal under all other relations. In fact no principle is better known among the ancients. Let us cite a single very striking example from Sophocles (Oed. Col. 230): 'Ἀπάτα δ' ἀπάταις ἑτέραις ἑτέρα παραβαλλομένα πόνον, οὐ χάριν, ἀντιδίδωσιν ἔχειν (But one kind of deceits matched against other deceits, requites the feeling of pain, not pleasure).

A word on oratorical rhythm.[9]

We must conclude then that there is an oratorical (or rhetorical) rhythm, but that it is not what the ancient critics believed it to be — it inheres in words and not in syllables. They seem to have thought of rhythm as necessarily belonging only to poetry. When their ears were agreeably impressed they attributed the fact to a certain disposition of long and short syllables, not supposing there could be any other cause. But Cicero himself who was a profound student of this subject admits that what is called a rhythmic style in prose is not always the result of rhythm or metre properly so called. His remark is found in *Orat.* chap. 59. *Idque quod numerosum in oratione dicitur non semper numero fit.* He is unquestionably right; for how on any other supposition, can we account for the harmony of Greek and Latin prose even now so sensible to us who hardly take any note of the quantity of the syllables? Hazardous as it may seem, I venture to propose some modifications of the ancient doctrine of oratorical rhythm. It seems to me that it impresses us not only by the detail of longs and shorts, but also by the arrangement of words sometimes more, sometimes less emphasized.[10] Nevertheless I do not dispute anything the ancients have said; the quantity of syllables counts for a great deal in oratorical rhythm. We have seen that it is not only the sense, but also the body of the word which exerts an influence on its emphasis. The longer a word is the more its emphasis will gain in force, other things being equal. This is true not only of French, but of modern languages generally, and it is therefore the more reasonable to suppose the same to be true of the ancient languages. But aside from quantity and metrical feet properly so called there is another element of which account must be taken in order to explain this harmony which is common to all languages, which every one feels and which is called by a name borrowed from the ancients — oratorical rhythm.

False emphasis.

According to our explanation, then, the order of words in ancient writers is in great part the cause of the music of their declamation. This or that passage in Greek or Latin may be said to be well written when the author has recited it well mentally; badly written on the contrary because the author has followed a false system of accentuation. In fact, to read certain passages from Hegesias and his school, cited by the ancient critics as examples of a false and affected style, we seem to be listening to a man who would be likely to emphasize at random. Dionysius of Halicarnassus, in Chap. 4 of his book *de Compositione verborum*, uses a passage from Herodotus to point out even in the simplest sentence the importance of the order of words, and the influence of this order upon the sense. Without changing the terms, but simply by transposing them in various ways, he has known how to mark the differences of style which characterize Thucydides and Hegesias. Imitating the style of the latter he writes, Ἀλυάττου μὲν υἱὸς ἦν Κροῖσος, γένος δὲ Λυδὸς, τῶν ἐντὸς Ἅλυος ποταμοῦ τύραννος ἐθνῶν. The name of Alyattes which is placed first in the sentence and followed by the particle μὲν is pronounced with a strong emphasis which does not belong to it. If the writer wished to call attention to the paternity of a son of Caesar or of Alexander this introduction of a sentence would be well enough. When Portia wishes to show to her husband that she is worthy of him, she addresses him with Ἐγὼ, βροῦτε, Κάτωνος οὖσα θυγάτηρ εἰς τὸν σὸν ἐδόθην οἶκον (Plut. Brut. chap. 13). Even if Alyattes had been a very illustrious father, the writer is not here making a panegyric but recording a genealogy. If the name of Alyattes is too prominent that of Croesus is too delitescent, and it would merit this place only if it had been named before and were repeated here merely for the sake of clearness. The word τύραννος is also badly placed in the middle of a complex term: τῶν ἐντὸς Ἅλυος ποταμοῦ ἐθνῶν. These three brief phrases answer the question about Croesus: who is his father? what is his native country? what empire did he govern? υἱός, γένος and τύραννος are the three points of departure, the three outlines to fill up. It is a singular affectation and at the same time a sin against lucidity to place the third point of departure in the midst of the other words."[11] Finally the word ἐθνῶν, detached from its group, preceded by a pause and placed at the end of the sentence, attracts to itself a stress of voice out of proportion to its importance. Contrast with this vicious arrangement the natural one that Herodotus presents to us: Κροῖσος ἦν Λυδὸς μὲν γένος, παῖς δὲ Ἀλυάττεω, τύραννος δὲ ἐθνέων τῶν ἐντὸς Ἅλυος ποταμοῦ. The difference in taste between Herodotus and Thucydides is not considerable. Κροῖσος ἦν υἱὸς μὲν Ἀλυάττου, γένος δὲ Λυδὸς, τύραννος δὲ τῶν ἐντὸς Ἅλυος ποταμοῦ ἐθνῶν. May we not suppose that the later writer purposely presented the facts given by his predecessor in a slightly different order so as not to incur the charge of having copied them? The forward movement of the sentence is a little more regular in the latter arrangement since the points of departure in the subordinate clauses stand first. The movement of Herodotus is a little more deliberate, more natural, perhaps. Not until he has said, Κροῖσος ἦν Λυδός does he proceed carefully to arrange the divers attributes of Croesus from three points of view. Finally, to speak of all the divergences of expression, τῶν ἐντὸς Ἅλυος ποταμοῦ ἐθνῶν is more round, more *one;* the arrangement ἐθνῶν τῶν ἐντὸς Ἅλυος ποταμοῦ is looser and more free and easy. Dionysius has proposed similar changes in the rest of this sentence, but we dare not protract an analysis that has no longer the excuse of necessity.

---

[1] My friend Benloew (*De l'accentuation dans les langues indo-européennes*, p. 216 ff.) does not admit the existence of the emphasis here spoken of, in the ancient languages. He believes that the Greeks and Romans supplied the place of the oratorical emphasis by oratorical numbers or rhythm. In the thesis above named he certainly maintains this view with great learning and ability. But has he proved his point? I confess that his arguments have not convinced me and that I am still of the contrary opinion. The very pages of Cicero and Demosthenes tell us, it seems to me, how they want to be declaimed. Every one of their sentences attests as I believe the presence, the energy of the oratorical accent. Try to read a Greek or Latin selection: if you do not indicate by your delivery the relation of correlative terms, though they may be at great distances from one another, you will hardly be understood. But have not the ancients spoken of oratorical emphasis? In several chapters of his first Book Quintilian indicates the method to be pursued in order to teach children to read and write Latin correctly (*emendate loquendi scribendique partes*). Therein he mentions among other things certain difficulties, though not many, which the tonic accent may produce in proper names, Greek words, etc. (I, v. 22–31). Then he continues in chap. 8, *Superest lectio: in qua puer ut sciat, ubi suspendere spiritum debeat, quo loco versum distinguere, ubi claudatur sensus, unde incipiat, quando attollenda vel summittenda sit vox, quo quidque flexu quid lentius, celerius, concitatius, lenius dicendum demonstrari nisi in opere ipso non potest.* (Reading still remains. That a boy may know in this where to hold his breath; in what place to divide a verse; where the sense is complete; when to raise or lower his voice; what should be read with a modulation of the voice; and what slower or faster, more excitedly or more calmly, can only be pointed out by actual practice.)

The words *quando . . . vox* seem to designate the oratorical accent. M. Benloew understands it to mean the tonic accent. Is this explanation admissible? Q. has discussed this accent in a former section. The accent of which he speaks here relates evidently, not to isolated words, but to the *ensem-*

ble of the discourse. It is necessary, says he, to note the pauses of voice, to indicate the end of a phrase and the beginning of a new one (*ubi suspendere ... incipiat*); it is necessary to mark the pathetic accent (*quo quidque flexu ... dicendum*). These are the first and third points that he illustrates. The second properly relates to the same order of things: it concerns the oratorical accent, and not the tonic accent. Is there need to call attention to the words *demonstrari nisi in opere ipso non potest?* Q. would not express himself thus in relation to the tonic accent, the rules and difficulties of which he has just pointed out.

[2] Syllables ending in an *e* mute are fem., even though the word itself be masc.; all others are masculine, though the word itself be feminine. Accordingly fem. rhymes are made with words whose ending is an *e* mute, and masc. rhymes with those ending in consonants or accented vowels. In neither case have these designations anything to do with the gender of nouns. See also note [5] below.

It is a familiar fact that a great majority of French words, perhaps more than five-sixths, is derived from the Latin. Whenever there is little or no written literature, and particularly when there is no systematic instruction in language, it tends to become more and more corrupt; or, to express the same fact in other words, it is subject to comparatively rapid changes. The influence of the various local dialects spoken throughout Gaul had a disintegrating effect upon the Latin. When a word is learned solely by ear it requires close and repeated attention to get it right. The accented syllable as the most conspicuous attracts most attention; next the syllables that precede this one.

Applying these facts to the transition of Latin words into French, all that followed the accented syllable was either not pronounced at all or neglected in the course of time so that the French word was accented on the final syllable. Thus it happened that the Latin word while undergoing the transformation into a French word in some cases lost all the syllables except that preserved by the accent. In hardly any case is that part of a word preserved which followed the accented syllable. For this reason French words have the accent on the ultimate. For example Lat. 'anima' became Fr. *âme*, 'villa' *ville*, 'securus' *sûr*, 'ille' *il*, 'debitum' *dette*, 'decima' *dime*, 'bonitatem' *bonté*, 'comitatus' *comté*, 'vitium' *vice*.

[3] To illustrate how largely the principles governing the order of words in French apply also to English it may not be out of place to insert here a few sentences from plain narrative. Scholars of course need not be told that the influence of French literature, or rather of French speech, became in time so great over the Anglo-Saxon with which it came into contact and conflict that the new language which arose out of the struggle and ultimate reconciliation resembled the French in the order of its words much more than it did the Anglo-Saxon. Almost every point that our author would illustrate by the French may be about as well served by the English. The following examples taken almost at random from Napoleon's *César* show that historical French may in many cases be turned into fair English by translating word for word and now and then transposing the positions of the adjective and noun. "Placés sur des hauteurs
    Placed   on   heights

presque inaccessibles, ces vastes ap-
almost inaccessible these vast ap-
pidums gaulois, qui renfermaient une
pidums Gaulish which enclosed   a
grande partie de la population d'une
great   part   of the population   of a
province, ne pouvaient être réduits
province not   could   be reduced
que par la famine."
but by the famine
" Quelle joie ne dut pas éprouver
  What   joy   must not experience
César en retrouvant sur les bords de
Caesar in   finding   on the banks of
l'Yonne son lieutenant, alors encore
the Yonne his lieutenant   then   still
fidèle? car cette jonction doublait ses
faithful for this junction doubled his
forces et rétablissait en sa faveur les
forces and re-established in his favor the
chances de la lutte." Similar exam-
chances of the struggle
ples might be got almost *ad infinitum*. We have seen in the examples from Joinville that in style the Old French was more like the Latin than the Modern French. The same is true of the English, and we need not go back so far as in the case of the French. There is a stronger resemblance between the style of Voltaire and Macaulay than between that of the latter and Milton or Hooker. There is in the later, particularly the ecclesiastical, Latin a tendency in the direction of what we may properly call a modern style of writing. Authors, whether they wrote in Latin or one of the modern languages, may in the matter of style be roughly divided into two classes: those who found their literary models in the past and those who yielded themselves more or less unreservedly to the analytical tendencies of their age.

⁴ The following familiar sentences from Chatham may be placed alongside these of Cicero. "A long train of these practices has at length unwillingly convinced me that there is something behind the Throne greater than the Throne itself." "If I were an American, as I am an Englishman, while a foreign troop was landed in my country, I never would lay down my arms, *never*, NEVER, NEVER." In the speech of Somers on the trial of the bishops as reported by Macaulay we have a good example of the effect of putting the most important word of a sentence first. "The offence imputed was a false, a malicious, a seditious libel. False this paper was not; for every fact which it set forth, etc. Malicious the paper was not; for the defendants had not sought, etc. Seditious the paper was not; for it had not been scattered by the writers, etc." But the system of tonic accentuation that prevails in English is the opposite of the French. The accent tends more and more toward the beginning of words.

⁵ Feminine rhymes are made by words ending in *e* mute. All others are masculine. The so-called *e* mute is often pronounced in French poetry, but not in prose. Many words ending in this way are derived from Latin feminines ending in *a*, whence probably the name. This final *e* makes a syllable, and should not be confounded with the final *e* silent in English. See also note ² above.

⁶ Quintilian, Inst. Orat. IX, 4, 20, *Initia clausulaeque plurimum momenti habent, quoties incipit sensus aut desinit.*

⁷ Compare the beginning of Xenophon's *Memorabilia* and the last part of note ⁴ above.

⁸ It is for a similar reason, if I mistake not, that both in writing and speaking persons employ a species of tautology to keep an idea, to which especial attention is invited, for some time before the reader or listener. "I, for my part, will not do it," does not

differ from "I will not do it." For a similar reason we say, "He himself did it." "Birds of the air," "beasts of the field," are simply birds and beasts. "Where in the world?" "How under the sun?" simply mean "where" and "how."

9 The expression which I have translated 'oratorical rhythm' would be more literally rendered by 'oratorical numbers.' The English writers of the last century especially, often apply the epithet "numerous," in the exact sense of the Latin *numerosus*, to both prose and verse. "Numbers" of course means poetic composition, but "numerous prose" is used of writings in which regard is had in the choice and arrangement of words to their rhythm and melody as well as their sense.

10 I have the more confidence in this explanation of oratorical number now that I find that it had already been made by Reisig (Vorlesungen über latein. Sprachwissenschaft) who distinguishes in oratorical number a "rhythm of thought and a rhythm of word." The two parts of the proposition which this scholar calls the "logical object and the predicate" seem to me to coincide with what I have named the *initial notion* and the *goal* of the discourse. W.

11 Dr. Campbell in his Philosophy of Rhetoric gives some good examples to illustrate this point. The Greek μεγάλη ἡ Ἄρτεμις Ἐφεσίων has been translated into Latin and several modern languages in the same order as the original without loss of vigor. But in the three French versions quoted a different arrangement is adopted with a great loss of vigor in each case. This goes far to show that there is a natural order of ideas to which words no matter in what language must conform. The quotation from Acts iii, 3, "Silver and gold have I none," etc., follows the same order in Greek, Latin, German, English, and in other languages. The Beatitudes put the same thought first in all the languages that I have been able to examine; yet the ideas could be expressed with grammatical correctness in various ways. Only native ability enables a writer or speaker to recognize that part of a complex thought which is entitled to precedence; education, to express it in the most fitting words. An expression may be made most effective by putting the most important word last. "In their distress my friends shall hear of me *always;* in their prosperity, *never.*" Pascal says, "The disposition of the materials is something new. In playing tennis both use the same ball, but one places it better than the other. It might as well be objected that I use current words; as if the same thoughts did not form a different body of discourse by a different arrangement, just as the same words differently disposed form different thoughts."

www.ingramcontent.com/pod-product-compliance
Lightning Source LLC
Chambersburg PA
CBHW031619170426
43195CB00037B/1211